The Promised Dawn

Advent Readings from Old Testament Prophets

Robert A. Gillies with David A. Stout

All rights reserved

No part of this publication may be reproduced, stored in a retrieval system, or transmitted in any form by any means, electronic, mechanical, photocopying, recording or otherwise, without the prior permission of
The Handsel Press Ltd

British Library Cataloguing in Publication Data:
a catalogue record for this publication
is available from the British Library

ISBN   978-1-912052-82-0

© Robert A. Gillies 2023

The right of Robert A. Gillies to be identified
as the author of this work has been asserted by him
in accordance with the Copyright, Designs and Patents Act 1988

Typeset in 11.5pt Minion Pro at Haddington, Scotland

Thanks are expressed to the
Drummond Trust, 3 Pitt Terrace, Stirling, UK,
for assistance with the publication of this book.

Cover Photograph
'Light and Dark Sky IV' by Robert Gillies

Printing and cover design by
West Port Print and Design, St Andrews

Contents

Acknowledgements	iv
Introduction	v
PART ONE – A Four Week Devotional Reading Companion	1
Week One	2
Week Two	25
Week Three	48
Week Four	69
PART TWO – Background Notes to our ancestors, the prophets	89
Isaiah	90
Amos	97
Zechariah	104
Haggai	109
Zephaniah	114
Malachi	119
Micah	123
Bibliography	127

Acknowledgments

All scriptural quotations, unless otherwise stated, are from New Revised Standard Version Bible, copyright © 1989 National Council of the Churches of Christ in the United States of America. Used by permission. All rights reserved worldwide.

The excerpt from Alcoholics Anonymous, the Big Book, is reprinted with permission of Alcoholics Anonymous World Services, Inc. ("A.A.W.S.").

Permission to reprint this excerpt does not mean that A.A.W.S. has reviewed or approved the contents of this publication, or that A.A. necessarily agrees with the views expressed herein. A.A. is a program of recovery from alcoholism only - use of this excerpt in connection with programs and activities which are patterned after A.A., but which address other problems, or in any other non-A.A. context, does not imply otherwise.

Additionally, while A.A. is a spiritual program, A.A. is not a religious program. Thus, A.A. is not affiliated or allied with any sect, denomination, or specific religious belief.

Extracts from Waves of God's Embrace: Sacred Perspectives from the Ocean by Winston Halapua, published by Canterbury Press are copyright © Winston Halapua, 2008, and are reproduced by permission. All rights reserved (rights@hymnsam.co.uk)

Copyright permissions for all other quotations have been sought where available and acknowledgment given appropriately.

Introduction

This book is an introductory companion to help reading the Bible. It has a deliberate focus and a specific purpose.

First, the focus. The intention is to read one short section from the Old Testament prophets each day in sequence over a period covering up to twenty eight days through Advent. That said, it can be used with benefit at any point in the year.

Second, the purpose. This is to deepen our understanding of the Bible, and to make a daily reading of it more familiar. The selected readings are taken from a sequence of Old Testament prophets.

This book is in two parts. Part One is at the heart of this book. It is the explicitly devotional section of what I have written. A sequence of readings is offered with notes. It will be seen that these notes contain anecdotes and narratives drawn from the daily life and ministry of either myself or David Stout. He has added valuable contextual prayers and reflections at the end of each day's devotional reading.

Part Two contains relevant background material on each of the prophets and the books of the Bible that bear their name. The historical, life and faith settings of our ancestors, the prophets of the Old Testament, are summarised in such a way as might add interest for the reader of Part One who is curious for something more. Questions of authorship and authenticity of what is given in the Biblical texts are considered and presented in a hopefully accessible way.

It would be good if, when reading these passages, you could find stories from your own life that make the Bible passages personally real. Likewise it might well be that you find something in them that helps you understand how God is working in your life just as you will see how God worked for those for and about whom the original texts of these scriptures were prepared all those years ago. You will find that David Stout's Hawai'ian touch adds particularly novel colour to the daily Bible devotions.

How you read this I leave to you. It may be individually. It may be as part of a group, or, for that matter, a combination of the two.

The Promised Dawn

Many friends and colleagues have given valuable assistance in the production of this little book. Their comments have greatly assisted its passage to completion. I am grateful to them for identifying deficiencies in early drafts of this text and which I have consequently endeavoured to put right in readiness for its publication. In particular I must mention with appreciation Dr Andrew Mein, the Revd Professor David Jasper and the Revd Michael Keeling for their comments on pre-publication drafts of this book. No doubt many shortcomings still persist and for those I accept full responsibility.

I was invited Revd David Stout of Hawai'i Island, Hawai'i, and the vestries of St James' Episcopal Church, Waimea and St Columba's Episcopal Church, Pa'auilo and their Beach Mass Community at Kawaihae, to deliver the annual Advent Programme for these congregations in 2020. Because of Covid pandemic restrictions I did this via a Zoom link from my home in Scotland to Hawai'i. The focus for that programme was a devotional reading of New Testament Epistles. This was followed by an invitation to deliver a Lent Programme, also via Zoom, in 2021.

I therefore acknowledge with deepest appreciation the further trust placed in me to deliver a second Advent Programme for these churches, this time in 2022. In doing so I recognise with thanks the immense generosity of those three host churches that enabled me to travel to Hawai'i to do so in person.

In preparing this second Advent programme I followed the pattern of the first; namely to give a series of addresses alongside a daily, devotional, sequence of readings from the Bible. This time my focus was on Old Testament prophets. The book you now have in your hands has been developed, with David Stout, from the time I spent through Advent 2022 in Hawai'i. I respectfully offer it as a second 'reading companion' to supplement the first.

The richness of that time in Hawai'i in Advent 2022 was immeasurable. So too was the welcome and the hospitality shown to my wife and I both by the members of those congregations as well as in the personal and personable warmth we experienced at every touch and turn throughout our stay on Hawai'i Island.

It is therefore to my supporting co-author Fr David Stout, to the vestry of St James' and St Columba's Churches, to their associate clergy the Revd Marnie Keator and the Revd Linda Lundgren, to the churches' administrator Jaisy Jardine, along with their congregations on Hawai'i Island that I am privileged to dedicate this second 'reading companion.'

+Robert A. Gillies
St Andrews, Scotland, Advent Sunday 2023

PART ONE

A daily reading from our ancestors, several Old Testament prophets, covering a full period of twenty-eight days of Advent, and being a preparation for Christmas.

Each Sunday – Isaiah
Weekdays in weeks one and two – Amos
Weekdays in week three – Zechariah
Weekdays in week four – Haggai, Zephaniah, Malachi, Micah

This daily devotional reading can be supplemented, if wished, with the more detailed background material that is in Part Two of this book.

Sunday – First Week

Today's Scripture reading: Isaiah 2:1-5

¹ The word that Isaiah son of Amoz saw concerning Judah and Jerusalem.
² In days to come the mountain of the Lord's house
     shall be established as the highest of the mountains,
     and shall be raised above the hills;
     all the nations shall stream to it.
³ Many peoples shall come and say,
     'Come, let us go up to the mountain of the Lord,
     to the house of the God of Jacob;
     that he may teach us his ways
     and that we may walk in his paths.'
For out of Zion shall go forth instruction,
     and the word of the Lord from Jerusalem.
⁴ He shall judge between the nations,
     and shall arbitrate for many peoples;
     they shall beat their swords into ploughshares,
     and their spears into pruning-hooks;
nation shall not lift up sword against nation,
     neither shall they learn war any more.
⁵ O house of Jacob,
     come, let us walk in the light of the Lord!

Digging deeper into the prophetic voice of our ancestor[1] Isaiah:

---

1   A note regarding the word 'ancestor' as an alternative to 'prophet'. My co-author, David Stout, added 'ancestor' here, and in many pages that follow in the material I gave him. This would be more fully recognised, he correctly considered, in Hawai'i. Arising from this and in email correspondence with a long-term friend, John Louch of Orkney, Scotland, reflecting on the use of the word 'ancestors', I wrote this:

"What has been a particular learning for me is the fact that in relation to the prophets of the Old Testament [the Hawai'ians] speak of them as their ancestors. We might prefer the term 'forebears' or 'forefathers' but the use of the term 'ancestors' signifies a deep cultural link between who the Hawai'ians are now and their 'ancestors' in the prophets of the Old Testament. It all makes for a profoundly different way of reading the scriptures." (5th December 2022)

Part One

It is always important to remember that when we read the Book of Isaiah from a Christian perspective today the original authors and hearers of the book did not. Jesus had still to come. We *look back* and, in faith, accept Jesus as saviour and look forward with anticipation and hope to his second coming. Isaiah, and those around him, *looked forward* to the coming of a Messiah.

The early Christians, who put together the New Testament, saw things in the Old Testament which convinced them that Jesus had been accurately forecast by Isaiah and the other prophets as that Messiah. From our perspective we can see how the ancient anticipation of a Messiah also fits in with the faith we hold that he will come a second time.

In these five verses, each one deeply rich in meaning, Isaiah has a prophetic vision of when God's peace will reign over all nations. It was a difficult time for them. These verses were written when powerful and aggressive Assyrians were seeking to conquer smaller nations whilst simultaneously Egypt was contending against Assyria. The smaller nations, whether on their own or in conjunction with others, were locked against the superpowers of their day; often violently.

I write these words for you at a time when war once more rages in Europe. Russia has invaded Ukraine and a coalition of nations, including Great Britain and the USA, are contending with the defenders against Russian aggression. To add to this, I could speak of violent regimes in war torn regions of sub-Saharan Africa and of frightening warlike rhetoric coming from the leadership of countries such as North Korea.

Isaiah's message of peace when weapons of war will be refashioned into instruments for harvesting food was as relevant when it was first written

---

Louch replied: "The wonderful insight of the Hawai'ian Christians, concerning their perceived ancestral relationship with the Old Testament prophets, has provided a flash of light for me that brings into focus the oneness, and timeless spiritual continuity of God's human family in Christ.

I wonder why I did not see this for myself – those messengers of God are no longer ancient, remote believers from a different race, and from a different place. This revelation has brought them as close to me as my own grandfather; the testaments merge, the covenants merge, and the whole is larded, so to speak, with a continuous family thread of witnesses, all with a common family identity and likeness." (8th December 2022)

as it is now. Moreover, the Temple in Jerusalem, dramatically situated on a high hill, is pictured as a place for the whole world to look up to. No other gods, whether those of stone or wood, or the gods of nationalist power or personal pride, or the gods of military hardware will be superior to the peace-making of the God of the Hebrews whom Isaiah saw as God for all people of all nations.

The peace which Isaiah prophesied was, for the earliest Christians, seen fulfilled in the person and work, that is the life and teaching, of Jesus. Christians, subsequently, also hold to this faith. Furthermore, faithful followers of Jesus anticipate that the failures of every nation, with their leaders and corrupted individuals who bring wanton violence on others, will be judged by God for failing to follow the teaching they should have heeded and the path they should have walked.

Just by way of interesting footnote, Isaiah 2.2-4 is quoted verbatim in Micah 4.1-3. It would seem that Isaiah's teaching and prophetic visions were widely known and respected at that time. Others clearly saw fit to use them in their own prophetic teaching.

Is Isaiah speaking a prophetic word to you, to our world?

Take sixty seconds of reflection: Choose a single phrase from the above passage and repeat it over and over again in your mind for sixty seconds.

Close in a prayer asking God for the peace of which Isaiah speaks and for the wisdom to discern (or heed) the path God would have you walk. Perhaps use the following prayer for inner peace . . .

> O Holy Spirit
> Free my thoughts
> From life's everyday cares and woes.
> Give me the courage
> To successfully overcome life's challenges
> And the wisdom
> To make right choices
> Bless me now with peace of mind. Amen.[2]

---

[2] Kahu Wendell Kalanikapuaenui Silva, 'Prayer for Inner Peace', *Hawaiian Prayers for Life Events,* Hawai'i Cultural Services (HCS), Kane'ohe, Hawai'i, 2020, 60.

PART ONE

Monday – First Week

Today's Scripture readings: Amos 1.1-5, 13-15; 2.1-5

1^1 The words of Amos, who was among the shepherds of Tekoa, which he saw concerning Israel in the days of King Uzziah of Judah and in the days of King Jeroboam son of Joash of Israel, two years before the earthquake. ^{2} And he said:
> The Lord roars from Zion,
> and utters his voice from Jerusalem;
> the pastures of the shepherds wither,
> and the top of Carmel dries up.

^{3} Thus says the Lord:
> For three transgressions of Damascus,
> and for four, I will not revoke the punishment;
> because they have threshed Gilead
> with threshing-sledges of iron.
^{4} So I will send a fire on the house of Hazael,
> and it shall devour the strongholds of Ben-hadad.
^{5} I will break the gate-bars of Damascus,
> and cut off the inhabitants from the Valley of Aven,
> and the one who holds the sceptre from Beth-eden;
and the people of Aram shall go into exile to Kir,
> says the Lord.

^{13} Thus says the Lord:
> For three transgressions of the Ammonites,
> and for four, I will not revoke the punishment;
because they have ripped open pregnant women in Gilead
> in order to enlarge their territory.
^{14} So I will kindle a fire against the wall of Rabbah,
> fire that shall devour its strongholds,
> with shouting on the day of battle,
> with a storm on the day of the whirlwind;
^{15} then their king shall go into exile,
> he and his officials together,
> says the Lord.

2¹ Thus says the Lord:
For three transgressions of Moab,
    and for four, I will not revoke the punishment;
because he burned to lime
    the bones of the king of Edom.
² So I will send a fire on Moab,
    and it shall devour the strongholds of Kerioth,
and Moab shall die amid uproar,
    amid shouting and the sound of the trumpet;
³ I will cut off the ruler from its midst,
    and will kill all its officials with him,
    says the Lord.
⁴ Thus says the Lord:
For three transgressions of Judah,
    and for four, I will not revoke the punishment;
because they have rejected the law of the Lord,
    and have not kept his statutes,
but they have been led astray by the same lies
    after which their ancestors walked.
⁵ So I will send a fire on Judah,
    and it shall devour the strongholds of Jerusalem.

Digging deeper into the prophetic voice of our ancestor Amos:

The Book of the Prophet Amos is one of the earliest in the Old Testament. Amos, as a person in the prophetic tradition, stands both in continuity with those prophets who preceded him (Elijah and Elisha for example) as well being different from them. As his predecessors did, he kept faith alive through difficult times. Amos, however, did not make his living from being a prophet, though was the first to write down the words that were given to him. He was, as verse one tells us, a shepherd and, as we shall in due course discover, also a vine grower of some substance.

In the years before calendars and diaries were invented and became popular people dated things differently. The details in verse one tell us a lot. His earliest readers would have been familiar with the respective kings of Judah and Israel and therefore of the reigns of Jeroboam and Uzziah. He speaks of what he saw two years before an earthquake. This earthquake

PART ONE

was also clearly familiar to those for whom he was writing, otherwise why mention it? Taking all these things together would have given his prophetic words a precise time frame readily accessible to those familiar with what he refers to. We do not have that ready accessibility.

However, we can do some detective work. We know that the King Jeroboam referred to in verse one reigned from about 787 to about 747BCE[3] in the northern kingdom of Israel. Uzziah reigned from the same year, or so, until about 757BCE, in Judah to the south. In addition, quite separate archaeological evidence from the region (at a place called Hazor) demonstrates a violent earthquake around 760BCE. We can therefore propose from all this a reasonable approximation that the date when Amos wrote was somewhere around 760BCE.

By way of detail, the name 'Amos' only appears in the Old Testament in connection with this prophetic book. Tekoa was a small village about ten miles south of Jerusalem. Standing on the ridge where this village once was, one would have looked westwards across the relatively fertile lands sloping down toward the Mediterranean Sea and eastwards towards the rocky, rough desert that takes one to the Jordan Valley and the Dead Sea.

The words, "Thus says the Lord", or "This is what the Lord says" (1.3, 1.13, 2.1, 2.4) indicate that what Amos wrote down came to him from outwith himself, from God in fact. They were not the product of his own preference. Further word repetition of the form, "For three sins . . . even for four, I will not turn back my wrath" (1.3, 1.6, 1.9, 1.11, 1.13; 2.1, 2.4, 2.6) gives linguistic force to the individual accusations the prophet ranges against those who refuse to let God be God. This is the standard form of prophetic address.

Fire is repeatedly given as the warning for the crimes and rebelliousness that are named ("I will send fire upon . . . etc") but amongst the actual punishments he refers to is exile (1.5, 1.15). Some one hundred and eighty years later, there was indeed exile to Babylon. Warfare and death are also signaled as specific punishments

Amos spoke his word first against surrounding rebellious nations and then, second, as we shall see in a moment, against Israel itself whose apostasy (namely, its betrayal of faith) made it as guilty as all the others.

---

3 BCE, Before Common Era, is the modern rendering of BC, Before Christ, and is the form adopted throughout this book.

It is as a person from the southern kingdom, Judah, where Jerusalem was, and still remains today, that Amos spoke the message from God, "The Lord roars from Zion and thunders from Jerusalem" (1.2). Jerusalem is the holy city of the prophets. It is not just what Amos said and wrote that gives him authority to say what he had to say. His authority also arose from the city where he proclaimed his message, Jerusalem. But, above all else, the authority of his message was secure because what he said came from God.

Is Amos speaking a prophetic word to you, to our world?

Choose a single phrase from the above passage and repeat it over and over again in your mind for sixty seconds. Is there anything about this passage that is difficult for you to hear? Are there ways Amos' words are calling you to examine your own life? Are there things of which you need to turn away from to be able to live a life more reflective of God's grace and love?

Close in prayer, offering up to God that for which you need to ask forgiveness so to help you move forward. Perhaps use the following prayer:

> Lord God,
> You made us in your own image
> and your son accepted death for our salvation.
> Help us to keep watch in prayer at all times.
> May we be free from sin when we leave this world
> and rejoice in your peace for ever. Amen.[4]

---

[4] From *Saint Benedict's Prayer Book*, Ampleforth Abbey Press, Ampleforth Abbey, York, England, sixth reprint 2011, 74. Copyright © Ampleforth Abbey Trust, Reprinted with permission and acknowledgment to Father Abbot.

PART ONE

Tuesday – First Week

Today's Scripture reading: Amos 2.6-16

⁶ Thus says the Lord:
For three transgressions of Israel,
    and for four, I will not revoke the punishment;
because they sell the righteous for silver,
    and the needy for a pair of sandals—
⁷ they who trample the head of the poor into the dust of the earth,
    and push the afflicted out of the way;
father and son go in to the same girl,
    so that my holy name is profaned;
⁸ they lay themselves down beside every altar
    on garments taken in pledge;
and in the house of their God they drink
    wine bought with fines they imposed.
⁹ Yet I destroyed the Amorite before them,
    whose height was like the height of cedars,
    and who was as strong as oaks;
I destroyed his fruit above, and his roots beneath.
¹⁰ Also I brought you up out of the land of Egypt,
    and led you for forty years in the wilderness,
    to possess the land of the Amorite.
¹¹ And I raised up some of your children to be prophets
    and some of your youths to be nazirites.
Is it not indeed so, O people of Israel?
    says the Lord.
¹² But you made the nazirites[c] drink wine,
    and commanded the prophets,
    saying, 'You shall not prophesy.'
¹³ So, I will press you down in your place,
    just as a cart presses down when it is full of sheaves.
¹⁴ Flight shall perish from the swift,
    and the strong shall not retain their strength,
    nor shall the mighty save their lives;

¹⁵ those who handle the bow shall not stand,
   and those who are swift of foot shall not save themselves,
   nor shall those who ride horses save their lives;
¹⁶ and those who are stout of heart among the mighty
   shall flee away naked on that day,
   says the Lord.

Digging deeper into the prophetic voice of our ancestor Amos:

Here, and following on from our previous paragraphs, Amos aims his challenge directly against Israel. This is a people that should have known better. Likewise, here in secularised Britain many increasingly refuse to let God be God. It is to us nowadays, as well as to people in his day, that Amos delivers God's word of warning and judgment.

Nevertheless, it is too simplistic to consider the circumstances in which we live and say that they are the same as those which confronted Amos. And yet, speaking at an entirely personal level, I cannot help but voice my own perspective. Let me say a little more.

The world is approaching climatic catastrophe as the oceans warm. Russia has invaded Ukraine and the Russian Orthodox Church gives crass and dangerous theological underpinning to Vladimir Putin's folly. In the past the United Kingdom and the United States have been caught up in military adventures no less mistaken. Meanwhile crops fail in sub-Saharan Africa and despotic regimes the world over treat their peoples with abject disregard if not utter cruelty.

I cannot say, with any certainty, that things are as bad now as they were in the days of Amos for every age has its troubles. But what I can say is that we ignore the warnings of Amos at our peril and the judgment that he voiced for Israel and its surrounding peoples may not be so very far from our door today.

Though most allegations against the nations mentioned here refer to crimes against people, with the only mention of sins against God being specifically in 2.4-5, it is quite clear from what is written that crimes committed against others are also crimes against God. The words of Jesus from the Gospel of Matthew (25.40) can be applied here, albeit in very different context, "What you did to the least of my brothers, you have also done to me."

Part One

In the original Hebrew of the Amos passage for today there is a series of conjunctions ('and') which link together the verses with increasingly deliberate linguistic impact of the sins mentioned. So, for example, from verses 7 and 8: "... *and* Father and son use the same girl *and* so profane my holy name *and* they lie down beside every altar on garments taken in pledge *and* in the house of their god . . ." Much the same emphatic structuring is also to be found in the best translations of verses 9 and 10. Verse 2.13 should most definitely begin with "Behold, I . . ." Whilst these may seem like small linguistic points they are in fact very deliberate emphases that should not be lost as we seek to be faithful in our interpretation of what Amos has to say to the churches.

Verses 2.13-16 stand against those who are rich and powerful and who think that either their wealth or their influence will guarantee them safe escape whether from the allegations which Amos makes or from the judgment he announces. The capacity of God to bring his judgment to bear is shown in verses 9-11 of this chapter. We will do well to heed this ourselves.

Is Amos speaking a prophetic word to you, to our world?

Choose a single phrase from the above passage and repeat it over and over again in your mind for sixty seconds.

There will always be things from our lives which we look back at and say, "I should have known better." Is there a decision you are making that the Holy Spirit is trying to tell you to listen to your gut? Does it feel like the Spirit is leading you to the better choice?

Close in prayer using asking for God's courage to follow where the Spirit is leading you. Perhaps use the following prayer:

God, I offer myself to Thee
    to build with me and to do with me as Thou wilt.
Relieve me of the bondage of self, that I may better do Thy will.
Take away my difficulties,
    that victory over them may bear witness
        to those I would help of Thy power, Thy love & Thy way of life.
May I do Thy will always![5]

---

[5] 'Third Step Prayer', from *The Big Book,* Alcoholics Anonymous World Services Inc, 2001. This prayer is freely accessible online.

Wednesday – First Week

Today's Scripture reading: Amos 3.1-11

3:1 Hear this word that the Lord has spoken against you, O people of Israel, against the whole family that I brought up out of the land of Egypt:
2 You only have I known
    of all the families of the earth;
therefore I will punish you
    for all your iniquities.
3 Do two walk together
    unless they have made an appointment?
4 Does a lion roar in the forest,
    when it has no prey?
Does a young lion cry out from its den,
    if it has caught nothing?
5 Does a bird fall into a snare on the earth,
    when there is no trap for it?
Does a snare spring up from the ground,
    when it has taken nothing?
6 Is a trumpet blown in a city,
    and the people are not afraid?
Does disaster befall a city,
    unless the Lord has done it?
7 Surely the Lord God does nothing,
    without revealing his secret
    to his servants the prophets.
8 The lion has roared;
    who will not fear?
The Lord God has spoken;
    who can but prophesy?
9 Proclaim to the strongholds in Ashdod,
    and to the strongholds in the land of Egypt,
and say, 'Assemble yourselves on Mount[a] Samaria,
    and see what great tumults are within it,
    and what oppressions are in its midst.'

Part One

^{10} They do not know how to do right, says the Lord,
 those who store up violence and robbery in their strongholds.
^{11} Therefore, thus says the Lord God:
An adversary shall surround the land,
 and strip you of your defense;
 and your strongholds shall be plundered.

Digging deeper into the prophetic voice of our ancestor Amos:

By now we are beginning to be familiar both with what Amos has to say and the way he says it. In verses 1-2 Amos speaks God's word against those of his chosen people, Israel, in the north. These are amongst those God brought out of Egypt. They have, so the charge against them goes, been every bit as guilty in forsaking their God as have all the other nations surrounding them in their particular warlike rebelliousness. Since the Hebrew nations of Israel and Judah were the chosen people of God they should, so Amos' word from God says, have known and done better than these other nations. Faith in God, and God's acceptance of us, as it did for the Hebrew peoples those years ago, carries serious responsibilities. Failure to carry these out has consequences.

The structure of verses 3-8 is forceful and deliberate. Amos asks seven rhetorical and colourful questions the implied answer to each of which is 'No'. This precedes his assertion that God does nothing without letting His purpose be known to those to whom He has revealed his word; namely to the prophets who interpret God's word to those around them. This comes as warning for getting things wrong as well as indication of the consequences when there is willful failure.

This is spelled out in verse 11. Surrounding warlike armies will serve as jury and jailers against the people of God who have behaved immorally ("they do not know how to do right") and cruelly ("they have stored up violence and robbery") in their "strongholds". Amos is saying that violent armies surrounding the people of God will be the instruments of punishment he uses against the chosen people who should have known and done better.

All this is potentially frightening and uncomfortable stuff. And yet, it is important to know that God will not simply ignore wrongdoing as if it had not happened. His day of judgment will come. The Gospel message of the New Testament is that the repentant wrongdoer can always return to God, like the prodigal son did to his father, and be accepted back in love.

Is Amos speaking a prophetic word to you, to our world?

Choose a single phrase from the above passage and repeat it over and over again in your mind for sixty seconds. Or: Sit in silence or quiet for sixty seconds and reflect upon what you have read in the bible passage.

A wise priest once looked at his congregation and said, "Christmas is God's judgement on the world. In sending Jesus, God judged us worthy of redemption. Know you are loved so much that God came to be with us, as one of us. Jesus then reaffirmed that promise by telling his disciples, telling us, "… remember, I am with you always, to the end of the age." *(Matthew 28:20)*.

Close in prayer asking for God for God's guidance and help to claim Jesus' promise. Perhaps pray the following prayer:

> Heavenly Father, in you we live and move and have our being: We humbly pray you so to guide and govern us by your Holy Spirit, that in all the cares and occupations of our life we may not forget you, but may remember that we are ever walking in your sight; through Jesus Christ our Lord. Amen.[6]

---

6 *From The Book of Common Prayer, According to the use of The Episcopal Church* (USA), The Church Hymnal Corporation, New York, 1979, 100.

Thursday – First Week

Today's Scripture reading: Amos 3.12 – 4.5

3^{12} Thus says the Lord: As the shepherd rescues from the mouth of the lion two legs, or a piece of an ear, so shall the people of Israel who live in Samaria be rescued, with the corner of a couch and part of a bed.
^{13} Hear, and testify against the house of Jacob,
    says the Lord God, the God of hosts:
^{14} On the day I punish Israel for its transgressions,
    I will punish the altars of Bethel,
and the horns of the altar shall be cut off
    and fall to the ground.
^{15} I will tear down the winter house as well as the summer house;
    and the houses of ivory shall perish,
and the great houses shall come to an end.
    says the Lord.
4 Hear this word, you cows of Bashan
    who are on Mount Samaria,
who oppress the poor, who crush the needy,
    who say to their husbands, 'Bring something to drink!'
^{2} The Lord God has sworn by his holiness:
    The time is surely coming upon you,
    when they shall take you away with hooks,
    even the last of you with fish-hooks.
^{3} Through breaches in the wall you shall leave,
    each one straight ahead;
    and you shall be flung out into Harmon,
    says the Lord.
^{4} Come to Bethel – and transgress;
    to Gilgal – and multiply transgression;
bring your sacrifices every morning,
    your tithes every three days;
^{5} bring a thank-offering of leavened bread,
    and proclaim freewill-offerings, publish them;
    for so you love to do, O people of Israel!
    says the Lord God.

The Promised Dawn

Digging deeper into the prophetic voice of our ancestor Amos:

Verse 3.12 begins with an allusion to the shepherding tradition of Amos' background. If a shepherd's flock was attacked by a wild animal the shepherd had to produce a piece of the animal that had been attacked so as to prove it was not the shepherd who had stolen the animal, or that he had been negligent. So, by comparison, if the nation of Israel is attacked by way of punishment for its wrongdoing and lack of faith, there will be only a few bits and pieces left.

The remaining verses of chapter three and the first five verses of chapter four continue the verdict of punishment against the faithless nation of Israel, under the name of Jacob. This is significant for it serves as a reminder that they are indeed the historic chosen people of God. Places of false worship (the altars, with their 'horns' – protrusions at each corner) will be torn down as will also the elegant places where the rich and powerful people lived.

In the UK we have what is popularly called 'celebrity culture'. In summary people become famous by being celebrities. They may not have done anything particularly worthy. They may well be nothing more than popularised 'bloggers', or TV personalities, or soccer footballers. But celebrity status is formed around them and people pay for magazines to read about them, 'follow them' on social media or watch TV programmes where they are featured. In short, these folks are famous for being famous.

It is this sort of idolising cult of the rich and famous that God, through the prophet Amos, is challenging here. And as if to taunt his audience into further wrongdoing they are invited in to what appears to be an orgy of wrongdoing in verses four and five of Chapter Four. Such is the sarcastic irony by which these wrongdoers are mocked.

Is Amos speaking a prophetic word to you, to our world?

Choose a single phrase from the above passage and repeat it over and over again in your mind for sixty seconds. Or: sit in silence or quiet for sixty seconds and reflect upon what you have read in the bible passage.

Part One

The word "worship" finds its root meaning in our "giving worth." When we come to worship, we direct our hearts to God – we give the value of our lives to God. As we walk these days of Advent, from darkness to light, how is God calling you to redirect your attention? Examine where you give your time, your energy . . . your worth.

Close in prayer perhaps using the following:

> I dedicate this day to You,
> O sacred Akua,
> The One who reigns supreme over the realms of
>   the heavens and the earth.
> Here I am, Your humble servant.
> On this day, I fervently pledge
> my heartfelt devotion to You,
> in thought, words and deeds.
>
> Guide me with Thy divine wisdom.
> Fill my being with Thy righteousness.
>   Shield me now
> from the causes of afflictions.
> Empower my spirit with Thy mana.
>
> Here is the prayer offering that I humbly
>   share in Thy sacred presence. Amen.[7]

---

[7] Kahu Wendell Kalanikapuaenui Silva, *Hawaiian Prayers for Life Events*, 24, (adapted DS), Hawai'i Culture Services, Kane'oha, 2020. Note: 'Mana' is defined by Silva as 'supernatural power'. This book is explicitly Christian but written in the tradition of Hawai'ian spirituality.

Friday – First Week

Today's Scripture reading: Amos 4.6-13

4⁶ I gave you cleanness of teeth in all your cities,
   and lack of bread in all your places,
yet you did not return to me,
   says the Lord.
⁷ And I also withheld the rain from you
   when there were still three months to the harvest;
I would send rain on one city,
   and send no rain on another city;
one field would be rained upon,
   and the field on which it did not rain withered;
⁸ so two or three towns wandered to one town
   to drink water, and were not satisfied;
yet you did not return to me,
   says the Lord.
⁹ I struck you with blight and mildew;
   I laid waste your gardens and your vineyards;
   the locust devoured your fig trees and your olive trees;
yet you did not return to me,
   says the Lord.
¹⁰ I sent among you a pestilence after the manner of Egypt;
   I killed your young men with the sword;
I carried away your horses;
   and I made the stench of your camp go up into your nostrils;
yet you did not return to me,
   says the Lord.
¹¹ I overthrew some of you,
   as when God overthrew Sodom and Gomorrah,
   and you were like a brand snatched from the fire;
yet you did not return to me,
   says the Lord.

¹² Therefore, thus I will do to you, O Israel;
   because I will do this to you,
   prepare to meet your God, O Israel!
¹³ For lo, the one who forms the mountains, creates the wind,
   reveals his thoughts to mortals,
makes the morning darkness,
   and treads on the heights of the earth –
   the Lord, the God of hosts, is his name!

Digging deeper into the prophetic voice of our ancestor Amos:

Once again we find the prophet, Amos, in full flow as he presses home his allegations against the people of the north. The things he refers to in these verses would all have been familiar to those for whom this message was intended. Even though they were punished for what they were, and had been, doing wrong the people had failed to heed the warning, had failed to repent and had failed to amend their lives. All of this they should have done. Not just because it would have been the right thing to do, but rather because God had explicitly called them to be His chosen people.

Being God's chosen people, and today this is us, means living God's life and showing God's way, to those who either reject God's call to them or who have yet to hear it. If any of us deliberately fail, whether as individuals or as a community, the call from God to us is to repent and turn again to the living God who, always faithful in love to us, will always accept us back to Him.

Some time back I wrote a letter to our church leadership as a response to its utterly awful treatment of a very dedicated and committed church worker. In that letter I wrote, "God will not bless the heart or the hands of those who have done this." All too predictably, though sadly, my words have been proven correct. God stands in judgment over willful wrongdoing and where there is a failure to repent and make amends then God's judgment stands. It may not always be evident, but it is there.

Verse 13 is like a creed; a statement of faith. It affirms and reminds us of who God is.

Is Amos speaking a prophetic word to you, to our world?

Choose a single phrase from the above passage and repeat it over and over again in your mind for sixty seconds. Or: Sit in silence or quiet for sixty seconds and reflect upon what you have read in the bible passage.

To Repent means to "turn around" . . . to head in the opposite direction. Advent is a hopeful time of year. The message is not to miss the Holy Spirit working right in our midst. Our congregation in Pa'auilo, Hawai'i, bears the name of St Columba. Columba literally turned his life toward God after making some seriously grievous choices. What an inspiration it is for us to bear his name for our congregation! We all stray from God's path, but we can turn around and find God standing right there.

Close in prayer using the following prayer attributed to St Columba:

Be a bright flame before me, O God
    a guiding star above me.
Be a smooth path below me,
    a kindly shepherd behind me
    today, tonight and for ever.
Alone with none but you, my God
    I journey on my way;
what need I fear when you are near,
    O Lord of night and day?
More secure am I within your hand
    than if a multitude did round me stand.
Amen.[8]

---

8   A prayer attributed to St Columba. Freely available in print and online.

PART ONE

Saturday – First Week

Today's Scripture reading: Amos 5.1-17

5:1 Hear this word that I take up over you in lamentation, O house of Israel:
2 Fallen, no more to rise,
   is maiden Israel;
forsaken on her land,
   with no one to raise her up.
3 For thus says the Lord God:
The city that marched out a thousand
   shall have a hundred left,
and that which marched out a hundred
   shall have ten left.[a]
4 For thus says the Lord to the house of Israel:
   Seek me and live;
5   but do not seek Bethel,
and do not enter into Gilgal
   or cross over to Beer-sheba;
for Gilgal shall surely go into exile,
   and Bethel shall come to nothing.
6 Seek the Lord and live,
   or he will break out against the house of Joseph like fire,
   and it will devour Bethel, with no one to quench it.
7 Ah, you that turn justice to wormwood,
   and bring righteousness to the ground!
8 The one who made the Pleiades and Orion,
   and turns deep darkness into the morning,
   and darkens the day into night,
who calls for the waters of the sea,
   and pours them out on the surface of the earth,
   the Lord is his name,
9 who makes destruction flash out against the strong,
   so that destruction comes upon the fortress.
10 They hate the one who reproves in the gate,
   and they abhor the one who speaks the truth.

¹¹ Therefore, because you trample on the poor
    and take from them levies of grain,
you have built houses of hewn stone,
    but you shall not live in them;
you have planted pleasant vineyards,
    but you shall not drink their wine.
¹² For I know how many are your transgressions,
    and how great are your sins—
you who afflict the righteous, who take a bribe,
    and push aside the needy in the gate.
¹³ Therefore the prudent will keep silent in such a time;
    for it is an evil time.
¹⁴ Seek good and not evil,
    that you may live;
and so the Lord, the God of hosts, will be with you,
    just as you have said.
¹⁵ Hate evil and love good,
    and establish justice in the gate;
it may be that the Lord, the God of hosts,
    will be gracious to the remnant of Joseph.
¹⁶ Therefore thus says the Lord, the God of hosts, the Lord:
In all the squares there shall be wailing;
    and in all the streets they shall say, 'Alas! alas!'
They shall call the farmers to mourning,
    and those skilled in lamentation, to wailing;
¹⁷ in all the vineyards there shall be wailing,
    for I will pass through the midst of you,
    says the Lord.

Digging deeper into the prophetic voice of our ancestor Amos:

    This is a long section. A key word in this section could be 'seek': "Seek me and live", "Seek the Lord and live", "Seek good and not evil" (verses 4, 6 and 14). We can read these as signposts for people to look for God in what is to all intents and purposes a funeral lament over the doomed people of Israel. Other signposts are in verse 10, for example, for here we find evidence that there were people in the northern kingdom of Israel who sought to bring people back to the God who will never desert them, even though in grief, God will punish them. In verse 10 we are told of how "the one who reproves" and "the one who speaks the truth" is disliked by the rich and powerful who lives in their "houses of hewn stone . . . with their "pleasant vineyards" (verse 11). These are they who "take a bribe" and "push aside the needy" (verse 12).

The use of a lament after things have gone wrong is something that is beginning to take root in the UK. It is easy to say what a 'lament' is not! It is not a confession of personal or community wrongdoing. Nor is it a punishment invoked upon one party in a dispute. Nor is it a negotiated resolution or mediation between conflicted parties. It is, rather, a recognition that in a difficult situation things have gone wrong. No fault is ascribed. No blame is admitted. All parties in the difficulty recognise that things should have been better; things should not have gone wrong. So, in a lament, all come together in the context of a contextually crafted liturgy in which all this is acknowledged. The following gives some illustration of two such situations.

Some time back I was involved in having to rescue a situation that had gone wrong in the church. Administratively and procedurally, we did all that was required. But we needed to do something else, liturgically, to express sorrow at what had gone wrong and offer prayer that things can get on the right track again. So a lament was prepared, based on the psalms, with careful instructions on how it should be conducted and was shared with all those involved. There was no confession of sin. But there was lament that things had gone wrong and, framed in the context of prayer with all those involved, there was resolve to put everything right – and to do so explicitly before God deliberately in a place of worship.

In another situation one of the two parties failed to turn up at the lament I had organized and agreed with each. We conducted the lament as had been shared in advance with all those involved. The failure to be present nullified any benefit the lament was designed to advance.

Is Amos speaking a prophetic word to you, to our world?

Choose a single phrase from the above passage and repeat it over and over again in your mind for sixty seconds. Or: Sit in silence or quiet for sixty seconds and reflect upon what you have read in the bible passage.

In the Rite of Reconciliation (Confession) – Book of Common Prayer of The Episcopal Church, USA, p. 447 – the penitent begins, "Bless me, for I have sinned." The priest then says, "The Lord be in your heart and upon your lips that you may truly and humbly confess your sins: In the Name of the Father, and of the Son, and of the Holy Spirit." The penitent then says, "I confess to Almighty God, to his Church, and to you, that I have sinned by my own fault in thought, word, and deed, in things done and left undone; especially _____."

Naming what we have "done and left undone" to a trusted person can unburden our souls. In the Rite of Reconciliation, the priest then pronounces the absolution, reminding you that God forgives you.

What do you lament? What do you list as a prayer of confession? You are always welcome to come to clergy for private confession. But you can also make your confession to God alone. Simply share with God what is burdening your heart and claim the promise of God's grace, mercy, and forgiveness. A word of counsel: Many of us have a hard time letting go, even of our guilt for wrongdoing, it may take you several times of claiming the promise of God's forgiveness. Close in prayer. Perhaps using the following:

> May the Lord forgive what we have been,
> help us to amend what we are
> and direct what we shall be,
> through Jesus Christ our Lord. Amen.[9]

---

9 Scottish Episcopal Church additional Liturgical documents: *Daily Prayer and Psalter.* (Undated but currently available both in print and as a download.)

Sunday – Second Week

Today's Scripture reading: Isaiah 11.1-10

11 ¹ A shoot shall come out from the stock of Jesse,
  and a branch shall grow out of his roots.
² The spirit of the Lord shall rest on him,
  the spirit of wisdom and understanding,
  the spirit of counsel and might,
  the spirit of knowledge and the fear of the Lord.
³ His delight shall be in the fear of the Lord.
  He shall not judge by what his eyes see,
  or decide by what his ears hear;
⁴ but with righteousness he shall judge the poor,
  and decide with equity for the meek of the earth;
he shall strike the earth with the rod of his mouth,
  and with the breath of his lips he shall kill the wicked.
⁵ Righteousness shall be the belt around his waist,
  and faithfulness the belt around his loins.
⁶ The wolf shall live with the lamb,
  the leopard shall lie down with the kid,
the calf and the lion and the fatling together,
  and a little child shall lead them.
⁷ The cow and the bear shall graze,
  their young shall lie down together;
  and the lion shall eat straw like the ox.
⁸ The nursing child shall play over the hole of the asp,
  and the weaned child shall put its hand on the adder's den.
⁹ They will not hurt or destroy
  on all my holy mountain;
for the earth will be full of the knowledge of the Lord
  as the waters cover the sea.
¹⁰ On that day the root of Jesse shall stand as a signal to the peoples; the nations shall inquire of him, and his dwelling shall be glorious.

Digging deeper into the prophetic voice of our ancestor Isaiah:

A new tree branch growing from the roots of the 'stump of Jesse' signals that the messiah, the saviour, that is to come will not be an earthly king such as was King David of Israel, or Hezekiah or one of the others nor yet, of course, one of our own leaders. This will be another type of king altogether; one who is directly of God and who will be God's saviour of the world.

The stump may be seen as the last surviving bit of the Hebrew nation, humbled and degraded by hostile surrounding nations. When Liz, my wife, and I moved into our house in St Andrews, Scotland, there was, in the garden a very overgrown bush that had grown over a pathway. In fact it was a very unpleasant thorn. Much as I tried to tame it my efforts were unsuccessful. So I cut it off right down to the roots. The roots had gone too deep and were too extensive to remove so I planted other things around where the bush had been in the hope that this new growth would be a good replacement.

Some three years later a new shoot emerged from that root amidst all the other plants that were by now flourishing. Even though it is a thorn, and therefore the comparison isn't exact, that new shoot in our garden is a personal metaphor and homely illustration of what Isaiah 11.1 is talking about. Despite every best effort to get rid of it, somehow it comes back. God is like that. People might try to get rid of God, but somehow God keeps coming back. Meantime, the renewed thorn is a lovely plant as distinct from the nasty briar of old!

That new shoot of which Isaiah is speaking is God's desire to bring a saviour amongst us, in spite of what we might do to ignore the fact. The qualities (or rather the God given gifts) the saviour will possess are wisdom and understanding, counsel and might, knowledge and fear of God. This 'shoot' will be God's saviour; Isaiah looked forward, prophetically, to such a person. We know, in faith, that person to be Jesus.

Jesus looked below the surface of things, deep into peoples' hearts and deep into the situation where people are held in repression, set apart by bigotry, isolated by human creeds of colour, race, gender or whatever.

Wherever opposition and hostilities are present now they shall be done away with. Verses six through eight contain wonderfully picturesque images of what God's will is to be and which we anticipate will come about when he comes in glory a second time in judgment on those who fall short.

That will be a time when words (echoing Isaiah 11.9) from Arthur Campbell Ainger's hymn, 'God is working His purpose out' come true, "Then the earth will be filled with the glory of God as the waters cover the sea".

By way of closing note we recognise also that the words of Isaiah 11.9 are also to be found in Habakkuk 2.14. It was clearly a significant thought for prophets looking forwards to the coming saviour messiah.

Is Isaiah speaking a prophetic word to you, to our world?

Suggestion for sixty seconds of reflection: Choose a single phrase from the above passage and repeat it over and over again in your mind for sixty seconds. Or: Sit in silence or quiet for sixty seconds and reflect upon what you have read in the bible passage.

Close in prayer. Perhaps use the verses from first stanza of Ainger's hymn, "God Is Working His Purpose Out", concluding with your asking God to work God's purpose out in you:

> God is working this purpose out,
>   as year succeeds to year;
> God is working this purpose out,
>   and the time is drawing near;
>   nearer and nearer draws the time,
>   the time that shall surely be:
> when the earth shall be filled with the glory of God
>   as the waters cover the sea.

Conclude by claiming the promise that:

> God is working out God's purpose in me. Amen.

Monday – Second Week

Today's Scripture reading: Amos 5.18-27

5 ^{18} Alas for you who desire the day of the Lord!
   Why do you want the day of the Lord?
It is darkness, not light;
^{19} as if someone fled from a lion,
   and was met by a bear;
or went into the house and rested a hand against the wall,
   and was bitten by a snake.
^{20} Is not the day of the Lord darkness, not light,
   and gloom with no brightness in it?
^{21} I hate, I despise your festivals,
   and I take no delight in your solemn assemblies.
^{22} Even though you offer me your burnt-offerings and grain-offerings,
   I will not accept them;
and the offerings of well-being of your fatted animals
   I will not look upon.
^{23} Take away from me the noise of your songs;
   I will not listen to the melody of your harps.
^{24} But let justice roll down like waters,
   and righteousness like an ever-flowing stream.
^{25} Did you bring to me sacrifices and offerings the forty years in the wilderness, O house of Israel? ^{26} You shall take up Sakkuth your king, and Kaiwan your star-god, your images that you made for yourselves; ^{27} therefore I will take you into exile beyond Damascus, says the Lord, whose name is the God of hosts.

Digging deeper into the prophetic voice of our ancestor Amos:

I have a friend who, quite recently, was taunted by a relative for not having succeeded in life. The relative has a very secure income from the rental of fourteen houses and apartments. Her husband has a well-paid job and they have a prominent place in the local community and church. Our friend, by contrast, is single, committed to each of the jobs she has had, and dedicated to help those others of her family who live nearby. She has an apartment that has an expensive mortgage and has been told by the rich relative that were she ever to have to give up the apartment through lack of money she (the relative) would not be offering her cousin somewhere to live.

This is a stark, typical and to my mind, quite cruel example of what is known as the 'prosperity Gospel'. In short, those who hold to this have contentment in life because they believe God has rewarded them for the things they have done and in which they have found material success. I find such thinking to be anathema.

Amos very evidently was confronted by thinking not unlike this for, with his vocal accent from Judah in the south, he rails against rich and prosperous Israel in the north. He charges those who think that by following the duties of festivals and solemn assemblies, by giving burnt and grain offerings, by taking part in worship offered in song and melody that they have done their duty before God. They have not.

Justice and righteousness are lacking. If these are not shared through kindness and help (to mention but two of the many possible virtues) with others more in need than oneself then any amount of ritual is nothing more than empty sham. One commentator has put it that "wealth cannot save" and that "human pride is destroyed".

The phrase 'the day of the Lord' which appears three times in verses 18 and 20 refers to the event by which God will bring judgment on those whose lives are based on such flawed expectation. Through adoption of the 'prosperity Gospel' its adherents assume that the day of the Lord will yield them glory in eternity. Amos, however, reverses this expectation. The day of the Lord will be "darkness, not light … gloom with no brightness". This is a hard message for us to hear. Mary's message in Luke's Gospel is relevant in this regard, ". . . He has cast the mighty from their thrones and exalted the humble and meek." (Luke1.52)

Is Amos speaking a prophetic word to you, to our world?

Suggestion for sixty seconds of reflection: Choose a single phrase from the above passage and repeat it over and over again in your mind for sixty seconds. Or: Sit in silence or quiet for sixty seconds and reflect upon what you have read in the bible passage.

A friend of our parish says an unchecked ego can become the anagram "Edging God Out"! Is there something you are holding on to that is causing for you to edge God out? Close with the collect (prayer) for the Second Sunday of Advent:

> Merciful God, who sent your messengers the prophets to preach repentance and to prepare the way for our salvation: Give us grace to heed their warnings and forsake our sins, that we may greet with joy the coming of Jesus Christ our Redeemer; who lives and reigns with you and the Holy Spirit, one God, now and forever. Amen.[10]

---

10 From *The Book of Common Prayer, According to the use of The Episcopal Church* (USA), The Church Hymnal Corporation, New York, 1979.

Tuesday – Second Week

Today's Scripture reading: Amos 6.1-14

6^1 Alas for those who are at ease in Zion,
 and for those who feel secure on Mount Samaria,
the notables of the first of the nations,
 to whom the house of Israel resorts!
^{2} Cross over to Calneh, and see;
 from there go to Hamath the great;
 then go down to Gath of the Philistines.
Are you better[a] than these kingdoms?
 Or is your[b] territory greater than their[c] territory,
^{3} O you that put far away the evil day,
 and bring near a reign of violence?
^{4} Alas for those who lie on beds of ivory,
 and lounge on their couches,
and eat lambs from the flock,
 and calves from the stall;
^{5} who sing idle songs to the sound of the harp,
 and like David improvise on instruments of music;
^{6} who drink wine from bowls,
 and anoint themselves with the finest oils,
 but are not grieved over the ruin of Joseph!
^{7} Therefore they shall now be the first to go into exile,
 and the revelry of the loungers shall pass away.
^{8} The Lord God has sworn by himself
 (says the Lord, the God of hosts):
I abhor the pride of Jacob
 and hate his strongholds;
 and I will deliver up the city and all that is in it.
^{9} If ten people remain in one house, they shall die. ^{10} And if a relative, one who burns the dead, shall take up the body to bring it out of the house, and shall say to someone in the innermost parts of the house, 'Is anyone else with you?' the answer will come, 'No.' Then the relative[s] shall say, 'Hush! We must not mention the name of the Lord.'

¹¹ See, the Lord commands,
  and the great house shall be shattered to bits,
  and the little house to pieces.
¹² Do horses run on rocks?
  Does one plough the sea with oxen?
But you have turned justice into poison
  and the fruit of righteousness into wormwood—
¹³ you who rejoice in Lo-debar,
  who say, 'Have we not by our own strength
  taken Karnaim for ourselves?'
¹⁴ Indeed, I am raising up against you a nation,
  O house of Israel, says the Lord, the God of hosts,
and they shall oppress you from Lebo-hamath
  to the Wadi Arabah.

Digging deeper into the prophetic voice of our ancestor Amos:

The same themes are continued in these verses from those in the previous reflection. Amos develops his charge against those who feel that their success in life will bring reward from God. Despite their luxury-living and their facility to dictate social and political outcomes as well as to enact society's moral codes God will grant them no favour.

As I write these words at the end of September 2022 I cannot but help comment on the current political climate in the United Kingdom. To confront a winter of rising heating costs, to combat rising inflation, to address wage inflation and to help pay for the war in Ukraine a ("semi") budget was announced on September 23rd which reduced taxes and reduced a national insurance payment that was, if I understand things correctly, originally designed to assist care for the elderly and housebound. I accept that some buoyancy has been given to help heating, cooking and lighting bills but the effect of what our government 'cack-handedly' did has generated world-wide criticism. Nothing was said to show how these tax cuts and national insurance payments were to be paid for. Clearly the rich and powerful will be better off. The corollary is that the poor will not be. In the meantime, the UK economy went completely off the rails of secure management and fiscal responsibility. Little wonder that the then new

PART ONE

Prime Minister and her Chancellor of the Exchequer were ousted within very few weeks of taking office.

Even though, since then, things have stabilized somewhat, if any nation ever needed an Amos to rail against it, it is my own United Kingdom now. And yet, through the years since his ancient text was put forth Amos has voiced God's word against those who lavish wealth upon wealth, and use power to raise the powerful to ever greater levels of human self-reliance.

The message and warning of Amos is unrelenting. An enemy will be raised by God against those who have denied extending His justice and righteousness to those most in need. Luke's Gospel again, ". . . he has filled the hungry with good things, and sent the rich away empty." (Luke 1.53)

Is Amos speaking a prophetic word to you, to our world?

Suggestion for sixty seconds of reflection: Choose a single phrase from the above passage and repeat it over and over again in your mind for sixty seconds. Or: Sit in silence or quiet for sixty seconds and reflect upon what you have read in the bible passage.

During Advent we "wait for the light." But we must be willing to open our eyes to see where God's light is shining. Close with this prayer, entitled "Help Us To See . . ."

> Help us not to fool ourselves with words, God,
> with talk of being sorry when we are not sorry,
> with talk of sacrifice when we have no intention
> of sacrificing, with talk of action when we are
> too lazy to act.
>
> Where our vision is dim, help us to see.
> Where our hearts are imprisoned by fears,
> release them. And when we see and feel
> your truth, give us the courage to act. Amen.[11]

---

11   Avery Brooke, *Plain Prayers in a Complicated World,* Cowley Publications, Cambridge, Boston, Massachusetts, © Avery Brooke, 1993, 85.

Wednesday – Second Week

Today's Scripture reading: Amos 7.1-9

7[1] This is what the Lord God showed me: he was forming locusts at the time the latter growth began to sprout (it was the latter growth after the king's mowings). [2] When they had finished eating the grass of the land, I said,
'O Lord God, forgive, I beg you!
    How can Jacob stand?
    He is so small!'
[3] The Lord relented concerning this;
    'It shall not be,' said the Lord.
[4] This is what the Lord God showed me: the Lord God was calling for a shower of fire,[a] and it devoured the great deep and was eating up the land. [5] Then I said,
'O Lord God, cease, I beg you!
    How can Jacob stand?
    He is so small!'
[6] The Lord relented concerning this;
    'This also shall not be,' said the Lord God.
[7] This is what he showed me: the Lord was standing beside a wall built with a plumb-line, with a plumb-line in his hand. [8] And the Lord said to me, 'Amos, what do you see?' And I said, 'A plumb-line.' Then the Lord said,
'See, I am setting a plumb-line
    in the midst of my people Israel;
    I will never again pass them by;
[9] the high places of Isaac shall be made desolate,
    and the sanctuaries of Israel shall be laid waste,
    and I will rise against the house of Jeroboam with the sword.'

Digging deeper into the prophetic voice of our ancestor Amos:

    The structure of these verses is interesting. They form a very stylised structure whereby verses 1-3, 4-6 and 7-9 each follow a similar pattern with significant repetition and with each echoing the others. In all likelihood what Amos said, arising from each of these three visions that came from God ("This is what the Lord God showed me"), has been deliberately shaped into poetic, perhaps even melodic, form.

Well over two thousand years later we cannot describe how, or the way, these visions came to the prophets though we do accept their validity. The vision of Isaiah 6 is another example of such. In the New Testament Peter's vision of the unclean animals as reported in The Acts of the Apostles 11.4-10 and the opening of the Revelation to John the Divine (1.9ff) can be taken as visions whereby God reveals something special to those whom He has called to receive such.

Thus far we have noted how Amos voices God's challenge against the people of Israel for every aspect of the way they have failed God. In these stylistically arranged verses there is a change. In these Amos pleads with God to change His mind about bringing upon His people a punishing judgment. Since "Jacob" (Amos' favourite name for 'Israel') "is so small" ... How can he stand" Amos first asks God to "forgive" His people (verse 2) and remove the devouring locusts from their crops. Amos next asks God to "cease" a "shower of fire" that would consume both land and sea. God, hearing the plea of Amos, relents and responds, "... it shall not be ..."

The third vision, though structured in a very similar way, does not contain a plea from Amos. Rather it pictures God's response to what will happen to Israel as God watches over it. A 'plumbline' will be placed against it. Used by builders, plumblines are cords with a weight attached at the end. When placed against the vertical side of a structure, such as a wall for example, it can be seen if the building is 'out of true', or is not straight.

So, God will place His plumbline against the nation of Israel. When they are 'out of true' then God will enforce his remedy, his judgment. In the way of things in that time judgment for wrongdoing was little less than violent.

Interestingly, Amos' visions are very homely and normal - a plumbline, a basket of fruit. Things that might just be around one's house, particularly the plumbline if work is being done on it, These everyday illustrations force you to think about the significance of what Amos is showing to us that, otherwise, we might easily not even notice.

Is Amos speaking a prophetic word to you, to our world?

Suggestion for sixty seconds of reflection: Choose a single phrase from the above passage and repeat it over and over again in your mind for sixty seconds. Or: Sit in silence or quiet for sixty seconds and reflect upon what you have read in the bible passage.

Close using the following "Plumbline Prayer" . . .

> Amazing and merciful God, how easy it is for us to forget that we are your delight. You we rejoice when we follow your holy ways and envision a future of goodness and grace for all your people. We blame you for divisions and strife. We justify our wars by saying that you are on our side. We rationalize the abuse of our enemies by telling ourselves that they are not your people, that their sinfulness exceeds your tolerance. In truth, you have told us that we are to love our neighbors indiscriminately. Moreover, we are to love those with the greatest need more fiercely and more immediately. Shower us with your mercy, O God, until we live by the plumb line you have repeatedly dropped in our midst. Amen.[12]

---

12 This above is part of a prayer entitled "A Plumb Line Prayer" by Rachael Keefe at BeachTheology.com. (The 'Amen' has been added, D.S.)

Thursday – Second Week

Today's Scripture reading: Amos 7.10-17

7 [10] Then Amaziah, the priest of Bethel, sent to King Jeroboam of Israel, saying, 'Amos has conspired against you in the very center of the house of Israel; the land is not able to bear all his words. [11] For thus Amos has said,
"Jeroboam shall die by the sword,
 and Israel must go into exile
 away from his land."'
[12] And Amaziah said to Amos, 'O seer, go, flee away to the land of Judah, earn your bread there, and prophesy there; [13] but never again prophesy at Bethel, for it is the king's sanctuary, and it is a temple of the kingdom.'
[14] Then Amos answered Amaziah, 'I am no prophet, nor a prophet's son; but I am a herdsman, and a dresser of sycamore trees, [15] and the Lord took me from following the flock, and the Lord said to me, "Go, prophesy to my people Israel."
[16] 'Now therefore hear the word of the Lord.
You say, "Do not prophesy against Israel,
 and do not preach against the house of Isaac."
[17] Therefore, thus says the Lord:
"Your wife shall become a prostitute in the city,
 and your sons and your daughters shall fall by the sword,
 and your land shall be parceled out by line;
you yourself shall die in an unclean land,
 and Israel shall surely go into exile away from its land."'

Digging deeper into the prophetic voice of our ancestor Amos:

Thus far we have seen Amos proclaiming God's grief-torn anger against the people of the north for their abandonment of the faith by which they were God's chosen people. In this section we read of the political 'kick-back'. Inevitably, what Amos was saying would not go down well with those against whom he was speaking.

Amaziah was a priest at the shrine in Bethel. He had a lot to lose should it be that Amos' prophetic preaching took hold amongst the people. So too had King Jeroboam. There was a history, among those people, of prophets' words and deeds toppling monarchies. Amaziah's report to King Jeroboam links verse 11 with the preceding verse 9. His rebuke is typical of those whose political space becomes inhabited by someone whose presence is unwelcome. The manner of rebuke is typical of such and in the UK can be summarised with the words, "Clear off and go back to where you came from!"

Amos' reply is interesting and offers an echo of what he said in Chapter one, verse 1. He says he isn't a prophet as such, but actually is a ". . . herdsman, and a dresser of sycomore trees."[13] He avers also that his father was not a prophet either. However, God has taken him from his normal way of life to speak what God requires him to speak to the people of the northern kingdom, Israel. Undaunted, the verses that then follow continue his volley – clearly directed both at Amaziah personally as well as Israel more generally. The term 'Isaac' (verse 16) is another term for the people of Israel; like the other term 'Jacob', it points to their historic call as the chosen people of God; a calling they have rejected.

In discussion on one of the evenings when I was introducing those present to the hard words of the Book of Amos at St James' Church, Waimea, one participant anguished that over-and-over again human beings get things wrong and nothing ever seems to get better. The same mistakes are repeated. Even though Amos gave his warnings and even though the people were given another chance still they sleep-walked into a calamity of their own making.

If I am to be honest it was this observation and the need to find a resolution of it that was the biggest challenge to come my way whilst preparing this Reading Companion. I kept coming back to the question, 'if wrongdoing keeps happening and subsequent correction keep failing what is it we constantly get wrong?' How can the cycle be broken?

In a totally different context the Orkney author and poet, George Mackay Brown, reflected on the same issue in a deeply woven allegory of God's purpose in Jesus set against the woeful inadequacy of human life:

---

13 The NRSV has followed the RSV by translating 'sycomore' as 'sycamore'. Here and throughout this book the change has been made to 'sycomore'. It is a quite different kind of tree.

'What has happened,' said the masked woman, 'is an old story. War. Conquest. Defeat. It has happened a thousand times. It is the story of mankind. The same old blood-stained tear-stained page is read, over and over and over, and re-enacted. Some day the finger of history may turn the page. On the next page, it may be, there will be a beautiful thing written.'[14]

Here in the remarkable and original prose of Mackay Brown we find human wayward failing exquisitely, if brutally, pictured. Against this, and from our Old Testament readings we find that, to give warning and direction God sent judges, kings, prophets and finally his own Word as the human person, Jesus. It was Jesus that the 'masked woman' referred to as, prophetically in Mackay Brown's folk tale, she foresaw His presence in the 'finger of history turning the page'. And then, continuing his lyrical vein, Mackay Brown prefigures the Second Coming of Jesus as God's final consummation and salvation of all as 'the next page'. Upon that page, when God's will finally overtakes human failure, 'a beautiful thing will be written'.

I like to think that my response to that lady in Waimea was as fluent and as rich as what Mackay Brown says here, but I fear it was not. However I offer this, now, as a response to her profound and penetrating question.

Is Amos speaking a prophetic word to you, to our world?

Suggestion for sixty seconds of reflection: Choose a single phrase from the above passage and repeat it over and over again in your mind for sixty seconds. Or: Sit in silence or quiet for sixty seconds and reflect upon what you have read in the bible passage.

How might God be calling you to be a prophetic voice? What injustice is God seeking to use you to draw people to see? Amos was a "herdsman, and a dresser of sycomore trees", yet God used him to call the people back to ways of justice and peace. Close using the prayer overleaf . . .

---

14 George Mackay Brown, *Andrina and Other Stories,* Polygon, Edinburgh 2010, 82.

God of the future, let those who negotiate for reduction in our wastefulness know your will. Reveal to us the real dangers of our impact on your world.

We pray especially for those involved in negotiations on:
    trade ...
        environmental policies ...
            affordable housing ...
                arms control ...
                      nuclear proliferation ...
                          climate change ...

Bring to us all a better understanding of good stewardship in our part of your universe. Amen.[15]

---

15 Rupert Bristow, *Only Connect: 150 prayers to aid reflection,* Kevin Mayhew, Buxhall, Suffolk, UK, 2009, 39 (adapted D.S.).

Friday – Second Week

Today's Scripture reading: Amos 8.1-14

8 ¹ This is what the Lord God showed me—a basket of summer fruit. ² He said, 'Amos, what do you see?' And I said, 'A basket of summer fruit.' Then the Lord said to me,
'The end has come upon my people Israel;
  I will never again pass them by.
³ The songs of the temple shall become wailings on that day,'
  says the Lord God;
'the dead bodies shall be many,
  cast out in every place. Be silent!'
⁴ Hear this, you that trample on the needy,
  and bring to ruin the poor of the land,
⁵ saying, 'When will the new moon be over
  so that we may sell grain; and the sabbath,
  so that we may offer wheat for sale?
We will make the ephah small and the shekel great,
  and practise deceit with false balances,
⁶ buying the poor for silver
  and the needy for a pair of sandals,
  and selling the sweepings of the wheat.'
⁷ The Lord has sworn by the pride of Jacob:
Surely I will never forget any of their deeds.
⁸ Shall not the land tremble on this account,
  and everyone mourn who lives in it,
and all of it rise like the Nile,
  and be tossed about and sink again, like the Nile of Egypt?
⁹ On that day, says the Lord God,
  I will make the sun go down at noon,
  and darken the earth in broad daylight.
¹⁰ I will turn your feasts into mourning,
  and all your songs into lamentation;
I will bring sackcloth on all loins,
  and baldness on every head;

> I will make it like the mourning for an only son,
>   and the end of it like a bitter day.
> ¹¹ The time is surely coming, says the Lord God,
>   when I will send a famine on the land;
> not a famine of bread, or a thirst for water,
>   but of hearing the words of the Lord.
> ¹² They shall wander from sea to sea,
>   and from north to east;
> they shall run to and fro, seeking the word of the Lord,
>   but they shall not find it.
> ¹³ In that day the beautiful young women and the young men
>   shall faint for thirst.
> ¹⁴ Those who swear by Ashimah of Samaria,
>   and say, 'As your god lives, O Dan',
> and, 'As the way of Beer-sheba lives' —
>   they shall fall, and never rise again.

Digging deeper into the prophetic voice of our ancestor Amos:

This is a long reading and is the fourth vision in the Book of Amos. By way of reminder we found the others in Chapter Seven, verses 1-3, 4-6 and 7-9. Two things stand out as worthy of particular mention here, though reading this passage in English it may not seem obvious why. Let me explain.

In verses 1 and 2 there are two mentions of "summer fruit" as well as reference to the "end". In the original Hebrew text of Amos these two words are very similar, and may well have been pronounced identically. The original word for 'summer fruit' is *qayis* and for 'end' *qes*.

We cannot say whether Amos actually saw a basket of summer fruit that led him to make a verbal link with such a basket that he might have seen in front of him in the shrine at Bethel and with the end of things for the people of Israel. However, it is tempting to think that he might have. Whatever the case, Amos then continues God's word against the people in a way, and with words, that by now are well familiar to us. God will never again overlook the sins of his people. God's judgment will fall upon them.

The assumption seems to be that the 'summer fruit' looks perfect, but actually is just on the turn - like a lovely bowl of apples but underneath, and out of sight, they are beginning to turn rotten. They are 'on the turn'.

Part One

Note also in the above passage the oratorical force of the repeated 'I will . . .' conjoined with the repetition of 'and . . .' in successive verses.

Is Amos speaking a prophetic word to you, to our world?

Suggestion for sixty seconds of reflection: Choose a single phrase from the above passage and repeat it over and over again in your mind for sixty seconds. Or: Sit in silence or quiet for sixty seconds and reflect upon what you have read in the bible passage.

St. Bernard says, "In those respects in which the soul is unlike God, it is also unlike itself. And in those ways in which the soul is most unlike itself, it is most unlike God." As the Revd Richard Rohr suggests, the pattern within the Holy Trinity is the same as the pattern in all creation. "And when you return to this same pattern, the flow will be identical" *(*from *The Divine Dance)*. As Amos prayed for his people, pray for the people of God and pray for particular Christian believers whom you know. Pray that the pattern of life for each may be more reflective of the pattern of God. The following prayer may be of help as you pray . . .

> O Great Love, thank you for living and loving in us and through us.
> May all that we do flow from our deep connection with you
> > and all beings.
> Help us become a community that vulnerably shares each others'
> > burdens and the weight of glory.
> Listen to our hearts' longings for the healing of our world.
> > [Please add your own intentions] . . .
> Knowing you are hearing us better than we are speaking,
> > we offer these prayers in all the holy names of God, Amen.[16]

---

16 Taken from the Revd Richard Rohr's 'Center for Action and Contemplation', Daily online meditations (2020). © 2020 by Center for Action and Contemplation, 1705 Five Points Road SW, Albuquerque, New Mexico, 87105. Used by permission of CAC. All rights reserved worldwide.

Saturday – Second Week

Today's Scripture reading: Amos 9.1-15

9[1] I saw the Lord standing beside the altar, and he said:
Strike the capitals until the thresholds shake,
 and shatter them on the heads of all the people;
and those who are left I will kill with the sword;
 not one of them shall flee away,
 not one of them shall escape.
[2] Though they dig into Sheol,
 from there shall my hand take them;
though they climb up to heaven,
 from there I will bring them down.
[3] Though they hide themselves on the top of Carmel,
 from there I will search out and take them;
and though they hide from my sight at the bottom of the sea,
 there I will command the sea-serpent, and it shall bite them.
[4] And though they go into captivity in front of their enemies,
 there I will command the sword, and it shall kill them;
and I will fix my eyes on them
 for harm and not for good.
[5] The Lord, God of hosts,
he who touches the earth and it melts,
 and all who live in it mourn,
and all of it rises like the Nile,
 and sinks again, like the Nile of Egypt;
[6] who builds his upper chambers in the heavens,
 and founds his vault upon the earth;
who calls for the waters of the sea,
 and pours them out upon the surface of the earth—
 the Lord is his name.
[7] Are you not like the Ethiopians[s] to me,
 O people of Israel? says the Lord.
Did I not bring Israel up from the land of Egypt,
 and the Philistines from Caphtor and the Arameans from Kir?

Part One

⁸ The eyes of the Lord God are upon the sinful kingdom,
    and I will destroy it from the face of the earth
    – except that I will not utterly destroy the house of Jacob,
    says the Lord.
⁹ For lo, I will command,
    and shake the house of Israel among all the nations
as one shakes with a sieve,
    but no pebble shall fall to the ground.
¹⁰ All the sinners of my people shall die by the sword,
    who say, 'Evil shall not overtake or meet us.'
¹¹ On that day I will raise up
    the booth of David that is fallen,
and repair its[a] breaches,
    and raise up its ruins,
    and rebuild it as in the days of old;
¹² in order that they may possess the remnant of Edom
    and all the nations who are called by my name,
    says the Lord who does this.
¹³ The time is surely coming, says the Lord,
    when the one who ploughs shall overtake the one who reaps,
    and the treader of grapes the one who sows the seed;
the mountains shall drip sweet wine,
    and all the hills shall flow with it.
¹⁴ I will restore the fortunes of my people Israel,
    and they shall rebuild the ruined cities and inhabit them;
they shall plant vineyards and drink their wine,
    and they shall make gardens and eat their fruit.
¹⁵ I will plant them upon their land,
    and they shall never again be plucked up
    out of the land that I have given them,
    says the Lord your God.

Digging deeper into the prophetic voice of our ancestor Amos:

(1) This is our final day with Amos! Today's reading falls into two sections, as indicated above. We begin with the fifth and final vision of Amos. As

before, it is violent and, to our minds at least, repulsively so. However, we must not read our gentility into the text and expect to see a mirror of ourselves and our preferences.

I know of two church-related situations where individuals behaved with appalling verbal cruelty (in my own testimony against the accusers I used the term 'brutality'). When one of the individuals who had meted out this treatment was the subject of formal accusations later on I found myself rejoicing at the professional suspension that then followed. This was my modern-day equivalent of that person being correctly treated with the same 'sword' as had been wielded so wrongly against others. Here, the emphatic use of metaphor can be very significantly useful in the way it leads the way to a contemporary understanding of ancient and more viciously violent language.

In verse 2, 'Sheol' refers to a sort of shadowy existence into which it was believed people passed at death before a final resurrection of the dead. Some scholars take verses 7 – 10 as the product of Amos' followers. Well, maybe. But only the last line or so of verse 8 is out of kilter with the rest of this book and probably therefore arises as the product of a later hand. I am inclined therefore to take what is given here as a whole to be the product of Amos' prophetic word.

(2) Notwithstanding what I have just written the remainder of the Book of Amos almost certainly comes from a later period. Two separate sections are marked by distinct beginnings ("On that day . . ." verse 11 and "The time is surely coming . . ." verse 13).

Both these sections (they are known as 'oracles') look forward to a time when all the judgment that Amos prophesied was to fall upon Israel would be past with everything restored to what it should be. Some one hundred and eighty years after Amos wrote Israel did indeed go into exile and Jerusalem, with its temple, was trashed. Verses 11-12 speak of its rebuilding and return to glory.

Verses 13-15 speak of how the people will have livelihoods refashioned into prosperity and comfort. Verse 15 ends, "never again shall they be plucked from the land that I gave them, says the Lord".

In so many ways, this is an ending of the type, "And they all lived happily ever after"! More theologically it is also a reminder of the conclusion in the

Part One

Book of Revelation at the end of the New Testament where, in spite of all that can and has gone wrong with our faithlessness, we still have that vision of the new Jerusalem when all that could be under God, actually becomes real.

Is Amos speaking a prophetic word to you, to our world?

Suggestion for sixty seconds of reflection: Choose a single phrase from the above passage and repeat it over and over again in your mind for sixty seconds. Or: Sit in silence or quiet for sixty seconds and reflect upon what you have read in the bible passage.

Is God speaking a word of hope to you? Perhaps it is a painful family situation you are facing, or some other difficult relationship. Is there a particular person who you offer in prayer to God? Amos proclaims the future that God holds. In your closing prayer, offer up your family and friends, particularly where there is tension and/or division. Perhaps conclude with the following prayer . . .

> Heavenly Father,
> Look upon our family with favour and forgiveness.
> We know that there has been tension
>   and tough words said.
> Help us to discuss, listen, and negotiate our way
>   to peace in the household.
> We try to keep your commandments,
>   but sometimes slip up
>   in properly honouring you and each other.
> If we can get our relationship right with you,
>   there is nothing that can stop us from sorting this out.
> Through the one who knew the difficulties
>   of family life,
> Your Son, our Saviour, Jesus Christ.
>   Amen.[17]

---

17 Bristow, *Only Connect*, 38.

Sunday – Third Week

Today's Scripture reading: Isaiah 35.1-10

35[1] The wilderness and the dry land shall be glad,
    the desert shall rejoice and blossom;
like the crocus [2] it shall blossom abundantly,
    and rejoice with joy and singing.
The glory of Lebanon shall be given to it,
    the majesty of Carmel and Sharon.
They shall see the glory of the Lord,
    the majesty of our God.
[3] Strengthen the weak hands,
    and make firm the feeble knees.
[4] Say to those who are of a fearful heart,
    'Be strong, do not fear!
Here is your God.
    He will come with vengeance,
with terrible recompense.
    He will come and save you.'
[5] Then the eyes of the blind shall be opened,
    and the ears of the deaf unstopped;
[6] then the lame shall leap like a deer,
    and the tongue of the speechless sing for joy.
For waters shall break forth in the wilderness,
    and streams in the desert;
[7] the burning sand shall become a pool,
    and the thirsty ground springs of water;
the haunt of jackals shall become a swamp,
    the grass shall become reeds and rushes.
[8] A highway shall be there,
    and it shall be called the Holy Way;
the unclean shall not travel on it,
    but it shall be for God's people;
    no traveller, not even fools, shall go astray.

⁹ No lion shall be there,
  nor shall any ravenous beast come up on it;
  they shall not be found there,
  but the redeemed shall walk there.
¹⁰ And the ransomed of the Lord shall return,
  and come to Zion with singing;
  everlasting joy shall be upon their heads;
  they shall obtain joy and gladness,
  and sorrow and sighing shall flee away.

Digging deeper into the prophetic voice of our ancestor Isaiah:

These verses are a development of what was portrayed in Chapter 34. That chapter spoke about God's justified anger against those who have fought against the people of God and sought to prevent their worship of God. This specifically refers, in the context of Chapters 34 and 35, to those nations and peoples complicit in the destruction of the Temple in Jerusalem in 587BCE.

Set against this background, Isaiah 35.1-10 looks ahead to that time when the whole natural world, and humanity within it, will rejoice that all things which are of God have become good.

Feeble hands, weak knees and fearful hearts will be strengthened. Blindness, deafness and disability will be overcome. Those who cannot speak and those who do not know the right things to say will have God's gift of speech given them. A clear path will be given so that those who know God can walk upon it in God's way with nothing to inhibit them and nothing that might otherwise cause stumbling.

More widely, in the natural world, the perfect Garden of Eden will be restored to where it was and to where it should be. The writhing tortures of the natural world which show themselves in flood, fire, earthquake, volcano and tsunami will be no more. Prowling animals seeking prey, malevolent individuals isolating the vulnerable and anyone putting themselves before God and his faithful people will either be no more or will have to face God's judgment.

The picture which these ten verses portray is of a time when suffering will be no more. When sin will receive its due reward. When all that is wrong will be put right. In one sense this is an ideal vision of what can and should be so under God's rule. In one sense only God can bring about what is given in this picture but, and it is a big but, there are those of us who can do more. Where we can we should. When we do we offer snapshots of hope that suggest what this vision might be like. Let me offer a few simple examples from the wider world stage.

When Nelson Mandela was released after twenty-seven years in prison as a victim of South Africa's racist governments his life as that nation's leader embodied forgiveness and charity. When Queen Elizabeth died in September 2022 tributes poured in from around the world testifying to her life of commitment, duty and service as founded upon her Christian faith. The queen did not always get it right, but – undaunted – she constantly learnt from her mistakes and sought always to give of her best.

So very often, and far too often, we fall far short of what God expects of us. First Nation Canadian people were appallingly treated, not just by successive governments, but also, amongst others, by the Anglican Church and the Church of England. Children were removed from parents and placed in 'schools' that sought to rid them of their historic culture. In such cases apology and where appropriate, reparation, is due for the wrongs committed. Credit is due to the current Archbishop of Canterbury for cutting through the philosophical problems associated with offering apology for things that other people have done. He extended to those First Nation Canadians an apology for wrong done them by the Church of England; rightly so.

After the second Sunday sermon in St James' Episcopal Church, Waimea, when I reflected upon Britain's sad colonial history and where we had despoiled and looted trophies from ancient cultures, and sometimes sacred artefacts, an Hawai'ian man spoke to me of his childhood in the 1950's and of how, even at a fee-paying private school where Hawai'ian identity was required the children were forced to speak English because that was the 'American thing to do'. He was not even allowed to use his Hawai'ian first name, his Christian name. Rejoicingly, a resurgence of Hawai'ian culture and language is now under way (having begun some fifteen years or so ago this man told me). He rejoices to hear his grandchildren moving effortlessly between English and Hawai'ian languages. I give thanks to God for what is happening today in the remarkable islands of Hawai'i.

It is in examples and instances such as these that we see God's kingdom coming on earth as it already has in heaven. In them we get a glimpse of the vision that is being shown us in these verses of Isaiah 35. It is in situations such as these, when lived by others around us as well as by ourselves, that we see God's perfect and future kingdom being made real in our time.

Is Isaiah speaking a prophetic word to you, to our world?

Suggestion for sixty seconds of reflection: Choose a single phrase from the above passage and repeat it over and over again in your mind for sixty seconds.

Close with the Lord's Prayer . . .

> Our Father, who art in heaven,
>   hallowed be thy Name,
>   thy kingdom come,
>   thy will be done,
>   on earth as it is in heaven.
> Give us this day our daily bread.
> And forgive us our trespasses,
>   as we forgive those
>   who trespass against us.
> And lead us not into temptation,
>   but deliver us from evil.
> For thine is the kingdom,
>   and the power, and the glory,
>   for ever and ever. Amen.

Monday – Third Week

Today's Scripture reading: Zechariah 1.7-17

¹⁷ On the twenty-fourth day of the eleventh month, the month of Shebat, in the second year of Darius, the word of the Lord came to the prophet Zechariah son of Berechiah son of Iddo; and Zechariah said, ⁸ In the night I saw a man riding on a red horse! He was standing among the myrtle trees in the glen; and behind him were red, sorrel, and white horses.

⁹ Then I said, 'What are these, my lord?'

The angel who talked with me said to me, 'I will show you what they are.'

¹⁰ So the man who was standing among the myrtle trees answered, 'They are those whom the Lord has sent to patrol the earth.' ¹¹

Then they spoke to the angel of the Lord who was standing among the myrtle trees, 'We have patrolled the earth, and lo, the whole earth remains at peace.'

¹² Then the angel of the Lord said, 'O Lord of hosts, how long will you withhold mercy from Jerusalem and the cities of Judah, with which you have been angry these seventy years?'

¹³ Then the Lord replied with gracious and comforting words to the angel who talked with me.

¹⁴ So the angel who talked with me said to me, Proclaim this message: Thus says the Lord of hosts; I am very jealous for Jerusalem and for Zion. ¹⁵ And I am extremely angry with the nations that are at ease; for while I was only a little angry, they made the disaster worse. ¹⁶ Therefore, thus says the Lord, I have returned to Jerusalem with compassion; my house shall be built in it, says the Lord of hosts, and the measuring line shall be stretched out over Jerusalem. ¹⁷ Proclaim further: Thus says the Lord of hosts: My cities shall again overflow with prosperity; the Lord will again comfort Zion and again choose Jerusalem.

PART ONE

Digging deeper into the prophetic voice of our ancestor Zechariah:

By way of introduction we need to note that the book of Zechariah is composed of two very distinct sections each markedly different from the other and each the product of a different hand. You will find readings from Zechariah Chapters One to Eight below. They are ordered and orderly unlike Chapters Nine to Fourteen which are not. We shall not be looking at these for they form no part of our Advent readings drawn from the lectionary.[18]

In the Book of Amos we found God warning the people of the northern kingdom, Israel, that He would use enemies surrounding them to punish them for turning away from faith in Him. Exile too would come their way as punishment. For them this exile was to take place when, in due course, the people were removed to Assyria.

It is very important when reading the Bible to see things as a whole. That is what we are doing this week. If, in our reading of Amos, we encountered dire warnings and threats from God (and these came to pass) so now in Zechariah we encounter a hope for a better future. Zechariah (and also Haggai, whom we will meet next week) spoke of a new future with a new relationship with God. It was a time when longed-for hope was being re-established. The people had returned home from exile. The Temple was being rebuilt. So too was the city of Jerusalem.

The people were returning to God and God would no longer desert them, but would return to them, "Return to me, says the Lord of hosts, and I will return to you, says the Lord of hosts. Do not be like your ancestors . . ." (verses 3-4).

Chapters 1 – 6 of Zechariah contain eight visions and Chapters 7- 8 four messages (or oracles) about returning to God. Our readings this week summarise all these.

---

18 By 'Lectionary' I am referring here, and elsewhere in this book, to the internationally adopted *Revised Common Lectionary*. This gives readings for use in churches throughout the world for Sundays (at communion services over a three-year cycle and at daily morning and evening prayer services over a two-year cycle). The Isaiah readings in this Reading Companion come from 'Year A' of the cycle for Sunday communion services. The weekday readings from the 'minor prophets' are drawn and adapted, in the main, from Year B of the cycle for daily prayer with some variations so as to enable a full twenty-eight days of devotional readings suitable for Advent.

Is Zechariah speaking a prophetic word to you, to our world?

Suggestion for sixty seconds of reflection: Choose a single phrase from the above passage and repeat it over and over again in your mind for sixty seconds. Or: Sit in silence or quiet for sixty seconds and reflect upon what you have read in the bible passage.

Conclude using the following prayer that highlights 'the Advent Hope':

> Almighty God,
> Give us grace the cast away the works of darkness,
> and put on the armour of light,
> now in the time of this mortal life
> in which your Son Jesus Christ
> came to visit us in great humility;
> So that, on the last day,
> when he shall come again in his glorious majesty
> to judge both the living and the dead,
> we may rise to the life immortal,
> through him who lives and reigns
> with you and the Holy Spirit, now and for ever. Amen.[19]

---

19 The 'Collect for the 4th Sunday before Christmas; Advent 1', *Alternative Prayer Book 1984, according to the use of The Church of Ireland,* Collins Liturgical Publications, London, 1984.

PART ONE

Tuesday – Third Week

Today's Scripture reading: Zechariah 2.1-13

2^1 I looked up and saw a man with a measuring line in his hand. ^{2} Then I asked, 'Where are you going?' He answered me, 'To measure Jerusalem, to see what is its width and what is its length.'

^{3} Then the angel who talked with me came forward, and another angel came forward to meet him, ^{4} and said to him, 'Run, say to that young man: Jerusalem shall be inhabited like villages without walls, because of the multitude of people and animals in it. ^{5} For I will be a wall of fire all round it, says the Lord, and I will be the glory within it.'

^{6} Up, up! Flee from the land of the north, says the Lord; for I have spread you abroad like the four winds of heaven, says the Lord. ^{7} Up! Escape to Zion, you that live with daughter Babylon. ^{8} For thus said the Lord of hosts (after his glory sent me) regarding the nations that plundered you: Truly, one who touches you touches the apple of my eye. ^{9} See now, I am going to raise my hand against them, and they shall become plunder for their own slaves. Then you will know that the Lord of hosts has sent me. ^{10} Sing and rejoice, O daughter Zion! For lo, I will come and dwell in your midst, says the Lord. ^{11} Many nations shall join themselves to the Lord on that day, and shall be my people; and I will dwell in your midst. And you shall know that the Lord of hosts has sent me to you. ^{12} The Lord will inherit Judah as his portion in the holy land, and will again choose Jerusalem.

^{13} Be silent, all people, before the Lord; for he has roused himself from his holy dwelling.

Digging deeper into the prophetic voice of our ancestor Zechariah:

These verses are very full of meaning. We can start with the 'measuring line'. This is given in Zechariah's vision, "I looked up . . ." (verse 1) Interestingly, the 'measuring line' can have several meanings – these being seen in the way that the term has been used in the original text of the Old Testament. It can, for example, simply refer to God's agent measuring the actual size of the rebuilt Jerusalem. It can also be a check on whether the people who now are inhabiting Jerusalem are 'measuring up' to what God expects of them. Additionally, it can also refer to the lineage of the people as descendants of the Hebrew nation of old. On this point I have often heard, especially in the USA, how people link themselves to historic Scottish clans (for example) 'I am from the McDonnells of Glengarry' or as one of my former priests proudly used to say when she came to minister in Scotland from California, 'My great grandfather was a Eunson of Fair Isle'. A person's heritage is their measuring line: where they have come from, where they now are, and what they intend to pass on. In the case of verse 4, what is being passed on is the re-inhabiting of Jerusalem.

A political warning is given to the people in verse 5. Whilst they may well want, or even need, a physical wall around them for actual security their real reliance should be on God who will be a 'shield of fire' all around them as well as being their 'glory within'. From the New Testament's Letter to the Ephesians we are reminded of how faith is pictured as a suit of armour: shield, breastplate, sword, helmet and so on. Ultimately, all these physical surroundings can be attacked and destroyed but in the end of the day one's integrity and security is provided by faith in God. A friend has told me the story of a colleague in Russia who, imprisoned because of conscientious objection to the politics of the state and whose practice of faith was restricted, continued to make the sign of the cross with her tongue inside her closed mouth when, had she made it externally with her hands whilst in prison, she would have been beaten.

God will come to dwell in the midst of his people who are summoned to come to live in Jerusalem, whether from the north or from the exile in Assyria. And God will be their glory. Note, and reflect on verse 13 for a few moments. "Be silent, all people, before the Lord". What a wonderful way to acknowledge God's glory all around us and within us. And pray also that God's glory will shine from us so that others may indeed see His glory shining from us both by what we say and by what we do.

PART ONE

Is Zechariah speaking a prophetic word to you, to our world?

Suggestion for sixty seconds of reflection: Choose a single phrase from the above passage and repeat it over and over again in your mind for sixty seconds. Or: Sit in silence or quiet for sixty seconds and reflect upon what you have read in the bible passage.

Close in prayer using the following prayer entitled, 'As Christmas Approaches'...

> Jesus, forgive us for being so busy,
> confused, and disorganized
> that we have little time to think of you
> as Christmas approaches.
> Help us to pause now
> and remember your coming
> to us and to the world. Amen.[20]

---

20 Brooke, *Plain Prayers in a Complicated World*, 56. (The 'Amen' has been added. D.S.).

Wednesday – Third Week

Today's Scripture reading: Zechariah 3.1-10

3 Then he showed me the high priest Joshua standing before the angel of the Lord, and Satan standing at his right hand to accuse him. ² And the Lord said to Satan, 'The Lord rebuke you, O Satan! The Lord who has chosen Jerusalem rebuke you! Is not this man a brand plucked from the fire?'

³ Now Joshua was dressed in filthy clothes as he stood before the angel. ⁴ The angel said to those who were standing before him, 'Take off his filthy clothes.' And to him he said, 'See, I have taken your guilt away from you, and I will clothe you in festal apparel.'

⁵ And I said, 'Let them put a clean turban on his head.' So they put a clean turban on his head and clothed him in the apparel; and the angel of the Lord was standing by.

⁶ Then the angel of the Lord assured Joshua, saying ⁷ 'Thus says the Lord of hosts: If you will walk in my ways and keep my requirements, then you shall rule my house and have charge of my courts, and I will give you the right of access among those who are standing here. ⁸ Now listen, Joshua, high priest, you and your colleagues who sit before you! For they are an omen of things to come: I am going to bring my servant the Branch. ⁹ For on the stone that I have set before Joshua, on a single stone with seven facets, I will engrave its inscription, says the Lord of hosts, and I will remove the guilt of this land in a single day. ¹⁰ On that day, says the Lord of hosts, you shall invite each other to come under your vine and fig tree.'

Digging deeper into the prophetic voice of our ancestor Zechariah:

This is another vision that came to the prophet, Zechariah. The person, Joshua, is not the same individual as accompanied Moses and the Israelites as they escaped from Egypt in search of the Promised Land. Joshua, here, is the High Priest in the Temple in Jerusalem. In these ten verses he serves two functions.

Normally, and when fulfilling his duties in the Temple the High Priest would be richly adorned in fine ritual robes. In this vision he is not. Joshua is seen, "dressed in filthy clothes". Beside him, so Zechariah saw in the vision, is Satan.

God rebukes Satan and affirms Jerusalem as His chosen place. God then affirms Joshua as someone 'taken from the heat of fire' to be his faithful priest. The deep symbolism of this passage then continues as God orders the 'filthy clothes' to be taken off Joshua. This does not refer to the actual removing of clothing but is a metaphor for the forgiveness of sins. Joshua, the High Priest, with all the sinfulness of humanity, as well as having suffered the indignity and alienation of exile, has this sinfulness removed as God's love and forgiveness pour over him. The forgiveness is visually pictured as new clothing is placed over him.

Yes, of course, this referred in a particular way to the High Priest. But it also referred, equally specifically, to the people returning to Jerusalem. All their past failings, literally their 'filthy clothes', were being removed as God clothed then with His new righteousness. As it applied to each person, so it also applied to the Hebrew nation as a whole. And it applies to us as well. God forgives our sins as we repent and our own 'filthy clothes' are removed and we are clothed anew by God.

The "Shoot" or "Branch" referred to in verse 8 is an anticipation of a future messiah. The given context for this is found earlier in the verse where the writer speaks of "things to come".

In the next verse is a reference to the "stone". We must remember that these verses are a single vision that came to Zechariah. In that vision Joshua, the high priest, is clothed with fine robes for his functioning in the Temple as well as a powerful sign of God's clothing of him in righteousness. A gemstone (echoes for us of the 'pearl of great price' in the New Testament), and more, would adorn that vestment and on it would be God's personal mark, his inscription, the 'autograph' of who God was, is and is to be giving the high priest his authority.

On the single day when the Messiah comes 'the guilt of all the land would be removed'. And on that day, all will gather under the shelter of the 'vine and the fig tree' in safety. Here in strongest measure, we have prophetic announcement of the hope of a coming Messiah, an ultimate high priest who would remove all sin and defilement as God's new clothing of righteousness is placed over all people and, yes, over us as well.

Is Zechariah speaking a prophetic word to you, to our world?

Suggestion for sixty seconds of reflection: Choose a single phrase from the above passage and repeat it over and over again in your mind for sixty seconds. Or: Sit in silence or quiet for sixty seconds and reflect upon what you have read in the bible passage.

Someone once said, "When thinking about life, remember this: No amount of guilt can change the past and no amount of anxiety can change the future." Close in prayer using a modification of an ancient Tahitian chant. Through God let your guilt pass away into the distance, praying...

>   I sail my canoe
>   through the breaking waves,
>   let them pass under,
>   let my canoe pass over,
>   O God.[21]

---

21   Winston Halapua, *Waves of God's Embrace: Sacred Perspectives from the Ocean,* 44, Canterbury Press, Norwich, 2008, (adapted D.S.).

PART ONE

Thursday – Third Week

Today's Scripture reading: Zechariah 4.1-14

4 The angel who talked with me came again, and wakened me, as one is wakened from sleep. ² He said to me, 'What do you see?' And I said, 'I see a lampstand all of gold, with a bowl on the top of it; there are seven lamps on it, with seven lips on each of the lamps that are on the top of it. ³ And by it there are two olive trees, one on the right of the bowl and the other on its left.'

⁴ I said to the angel who talked with me, 'What are these, my lord?' ⁵ Then the angel who talked with me answered me, 'Do you not know what these are?' I said, 'No, my lord.' ⁶ He said to me, 'This is the word of the Lord to Zerubbabel: Not by might, nor by power, but by my spirit, says the Lord of hosts. ⁷ What are you, O great mountain? Before Zerubbabel you shall become a plain; and he shall bring out the top stone amid shouts of "Grace, grace to it!"'

⁸ Moreover, the word of the Lord came to me, saying, ⁹ 'The hands of Zerubbabel have laid the foundation of this house; his hands shall also complete it. Then you will know that the Lord of hosts has sent me to you. ¹⁰ For whoever has despised the day of small things shall rejoice, and shall see the plummet in the hand of Zerubbabel.

'These seven are the eyes of the Lord, which range through the whole earth.' ¹¹ Then I said to him, 'What are these two olive trees on the right and the left of the lampstand?' ¹² And a second time I said to him, 'What are these two branches of the olive trees, which pour out the oil[a] through the two golden pipes?' ¹³ He said to me, 'Do you not know what these are?' I said, 'No, my lord.' ¹⁴ Then he said, 'These are the two anointed ones who stand by the Lord of the whole earth.'

Digging deeper into the prophetic voice of our ancestor Zechariah:

Much scholarly investigation has gone into what the seven lamps might have looked like. It is too simple to think they might be the seven branched menorah familiar to us in modern day Jewish homes and synagogues I intend to say no more about what they looked like. The fine detail of

Hebrew translation is not what this Reading Companion is about! For present purposes I shall interpret these verses allegorically even though, I admit, I am 'reading things into' the verses rather than 'reading what they actually say'!

'Being awakened as one is wakened from sleep' happens to all of us when God wakes us up from what a friend of mine described in a colourfully picturesque sermon as, "vacuous living" and gives us the wherewithal to see things from God's perspective.

And when we look from God's perspective we see lamps all around us, each one giving light to supplement the light which the others provide. We may read these verses as referring to those other people of faith in our local Christian communities who each, in their own personal and individual ways, give an overall ambience of light that surrounds each of us and illumines all.

Originally God's light had shone from the Jerusalem Temple, and in a historical sense this is what would have been inspiring Zechariah, but now from our perspective it shines from Jesus Christ. The light we see is his all-seeing light. It embraces all seven continents of our world and is there even in those locations where its suppression is attempted.

The seemingly curious insertion of 'Zerubbabel' into the vision from verses 6-10a interrupts the flow of the vision. Zerubbabel was the governor under whose authority the Temple was being rebuilt. "The hands of Zerubbabel have laid the foundations of this house [ie the Temple]; his hands shall also complete it". By this means the people, "will know that the Lord of hosts has sent me [Zechariah] to you." (Verse 9) Zerubbabel, the governor, has overseen the construction of the Temple and will see it through to completion.

The two olive trees symbolise Joshua the high priest and Zerubbabel, the governor. In their exile the Hebrew people had neither high priest or governor (king). By choosing both these to accomplish that which God promised in the rebuilding of the Jerusalem Temple the people would have been given hope that God was restoring them to the promised land. In Jesus we have both priest and king in one person and thus, in faith, we can see God has fulfilled his promise in the person and work of Jesus.

Part One

In the South Asia Bible Commentary Solomon Kumar writes, "Just as God used Joshua and Zerubbabel to build his temple and encourage his people, so today he uses us all, pastors and church members, to build his church".[22]

Is Zechariah speaking a prophetic word to you, to our world?

Suggestion for sixty seconds of reflection: Choose a single phrase from the above passage and repeat it over and over again in your mind for sixty seconds. Or: Sit in silence or quiet for sixty seconds and reflect upon what you have read in the bible passage.

In Hawai'i the wa'a (outrigger canoe) offers a vivid image of people coming together to learn to paddle as one. Each paddler must seek to keep their hearts and minds present in the rhythm of the canoe. The same could be said of a parish or church community (the Hawai'ians speak of this as the 'parish ohana'). The following prayer comes from a young person from the South Pacific island country of Vanuatu. As you say it, see not only yourself in the canoe, but those paddling with you.

> O Jesus,
> be the canoe
> that holds me in the sea of life,
> be the steer that keeps me straight,
> be the outrigger that supports me in times of great temptation.
>
> Let your Spirit be my sail that carries me through each day,
> as I journey steadfastly
> on the long voyage of life.
> Amen.[23]

---

22 Solomon Kumar, 'Zechariah', *op cit*, 1197
23 Halapua, *Waves of God's Embrace*, 15.

Friday – Third Week

Today's Scripture reading: Zechariah 7.8 – 8.8

⁸ The word of the Lord came to Zechariah, saying: ⁹ Thus says the Lord of hosts: Render true judgements, show kindness and mercy to one another; ¹⁰ do not oppress the widow, the orphan, the alien, or the poor; and do not devise evil in your hearts against one another.

¹¹ But they refused to listen, and turned a stubborn shoulder, and stopped their ears in order not to hear. ¹² They made their hearts adamant in order not to hear the law and the words that the Lord of hosts had sent by his spirit through the former prophets. Therefore great wrath came from the Lord of hosts. ¹³ Just as, when I called, they would not hear, so, when they called, I would not hear, says the Lord of hosts, ¹⁴ and I scattered them with a whirlwind among all the nations that they had not known. Thus the land they left was desolate, so that no one went to and fro, and a pleasant land was made desolate.

8¹ The word of the Lord of hosts came to me, saying: ² Thus says the Lord of hosts: I am jealous for Zion with great jealousy, and I am jealous for her with great wrath. ³ Thus says the Lord: I will return to Zion, and will dwell in the midst of Jerusalem; Jerusalem shall be called the faithful city, and the mountain of the Lord of hosts shall be called the holy mountain. ⁴ Thus says the Lord of hosts: Old men and old women shall again sit in the streets of Jerusalem, each with staff in hand because of their great age. ⁵ And the streets of the city shall be full of boys and girls playing in its streets.

⁶ Thus says the Lord of hosts: Even though it seems impossible to the remnant of this people in these days, should it also seem impossible to me, says the Lord of hosts? ⁷ Thus says the Lord of hosts: I will save my people from the east country and from the west country; ⁸ and I will bring them to live in Jerusalem. They shall be my people and I will be their God, in faithfulness and in righteousness.

Part One

Digging deeper into the prophetic voice of our ancestor Zechariah:

These verses begin with the form now very familiar from the last few days, "The word of the Lord came to Zechariah . . . Thus says the Lord of hosts . . ." And there follow moral injunctions about how to live a generous and thoughtfully kind life. Echoes of the Ten Commandments and the Beatitudes in Matthew's Gospel sound through very clearly.

Without any real connection with what has just been said verse 11 begins, "But they . . ." evidently linking what the author is about to say with the advocacy of good moral living he has just mentioned. We are required to make an intuitive jump one to the other. It would seem that the author is saying that the people had forgotten, or were ignoring, God's earlier kindness. The use of the body in verses 11-12 is interesting. In order we have, "a stubborn shoulder . . . stopped up ears . . . stony hearts".

Not too much need be made of this except to note that it is the whole body which is involved from the 'cold' shoulder (as we say in the UK), ear blockers and a stubborn heart thereby to obstruct the will of God. And as they shunned the word of God when He called to them, so God in His turn shunned them when they called to Him. With these words Zechariah is reminding his audience that this is what happened in the past.

Next comes the promise of God to be with his people. This prophetic word that came to Zechariah is by the familiar form of Chapter 8, verse 1. Zechariah voices God's love for Jerusalem and for His people. Each person will be safe and will live full and contented lives.

On the BBC news in early October 2022 there was an interview with a woman in war-torn, bombed-out eastern Ukraine. Her words were something like, "All we want to do is live a normal, ordinary life." When lives are shattered by needless and cruel warfare the normal, ordinary, routine of daily life becomes a cherished dream. The reality that this dream will come true is what Zechariah was prophesying. In our prayers we must urge the same prophecy to come true for the tortured peoples of Ukraine.

Is Zechariah speaking a prophetic word to you, to our world?

Suggestion for sixty seconds of reflection: Choose a single phrase from the above passage and repeat it over and over again in your mind for sixty seconds. Sit in silence or quiet for sixty seconds and reflect upon what you have read in the bible passage.

Close in prayer. Perhaps use the following traditional Gaelic blessing. As you say it, think of people and places, both far away and at home, for whom you are praying for peace:

> Deep peace of the running wave to you
> Deep peace of the flowing air to you
> Deep peace of the quiet earth to you
> Deep peace of the shining stars to you
> Deep peace of the Son of peace to you.
> Amen.[24]

---

24 A traditional Gaelic blessing. Freely available in published form and online.

PART ONE

Saturday – Third Week

Today's Scripture reading: Zechariah 8.9-17

^{9} Thus says the Lord of hosts: Let your hands be strong—you that have recently been hearing these words from the mouths of the prophets who were present when the foundation was laid for the rebuilding of the temple, the house of the Lord of hosts. ^{10} For before those days there were no wages for people or for animals, nor was there any safety from the foe for those who went out or came in, and I set them all against one another. ^{11} But now I will not deal with the remnant of this people as in the former days, says the Lord of hosts. ^{12} For there shall be a sowing of peace; the vine shall yield its fruit, the ground shall give its produce, and the skies shall give their dew; and I will cause the remnant of this people to possess all these things. ^{13} Just as you have been a cursing among the nations, O house of Judah and house of Israel, so I will save you and you shall be a blessing. Do not be afraid, but let your hands be strong.

^{14} For thus says the Lord of hosts: Just as I purposed to bring disaster upon you, when your ancestors provoked me to wrath, and I did not relent, says the Lord of hosts, ^{15} so again I have purposed in these days to do good to Jerusalem and to the house of Judah; do not be afraid. ^{16} These are the things that you shall do: Speak the truth to one another, render in your gates judgements that are true and make for peace, ^{17} do not devise evil in your hearts against one another, and love no false oath; for all these are things that I hate, says the Lord.

Digging deeper into the prophetic voice of our ancestor Zechariah:

In verse 16 Zechariah once again voices God's word for the way people should live: ". . . speaking truth . . . judge truthfully . . . and peacefully . . . do not devise evil against one another . . . do not love a false oath . . ." By so doing the people will honour God. The kingdoms of Israel (in the north) and Judah (in the south) will both be a blessing to God and to those nations around them.

These verses follow a reminder of God's rejection of those who had formerly rejected Him, but now as a faithful remnant they are brought back to the holy city of Jerusalem and it is they who will rebuild it – not to their own glory but to the glory of God. With this returning remnant there will be a "... sowing of peace ... the vine will fruit ... the ground its produce ... the sky will offer rain ... and all will benefit from this." (Verse 12)

Is Zechariah speaking a prophetic word to you, to our world?

Suggestion for sixty seconds of reflection: Choose a single phrase from the above passage and repeat it over and over again in your mind for sixty seconds. Or: Sit in silence or quiet for sixty seconds and reflect upon what you have read in the bible passage.

The following prayer was offered by the Presbyterian pastor, the Revd Bill Forbes. He wrote this to his friends as he was facing a terminal illness. It was offered with a certain spiritual clarity. As you read it, imagine it being said to you ...

> None of us knows how many days we will be granted. As you look into the mirror each and every day, take time to marvel that you have been created in the image of God. Count your blessings often... Share yourself abundantly with those who need encouragement, hope, and care... Keep that twinkle in your eye and help the world learn to laugh... May God continue to bless you and keep you as you claim the gift of life each day! Amen.[25]

---

25 This prayer was created and offered by the Revd Bill Forbes, in the weeks before his death, June 30, 2009. Pastor Bill served on the staff at Trinity Episcopal Church in Asbury Park, New Jersey, USA. (D.S.)

PART ONE

Sunday – Fourth Week

Today's Scripture reading: Isaiah 7.10-16

7:10 Again the Lord spoke to Ahaz, saying, 11 Ask a sign of the Lord your God; let it be deep as Sheol or high as heaven.

12 But Ahaz said, I will not ask, and I will not put the Lord to the test.

13 Then Isaiah said: 'Hear then, O house of David! Is it too little for you to weary mortals, that you weary my God also? 14 Therefore the Lord himself will give you a sign. Look, the young woman is with child and shall bear a son, and shall name him Immanuel. 15 He shall eat curds and honey by the time he knows how to refuse the evil and choose the good. 16 For before the child knows how to refuse the evil and choose the good, the land before whose two kings you are in dread will be deserted.'

Digging deeper into the prophetic voice of our ancestor Isaiah:

This is a difficult and complex passage to understand. I will try to make it as straightforward as possible. At the heart of these verses is the importance of 'choosing'. Deliberately, that means choosing that which is of God and of what God offers.

Ahaz was king of Judah. Plots were hatched by enemies to bring down Ahaz. Isaiah was instructed by God to speak to Ahaz and so gave him the message (in the second half of verse nine), "If you do not stand firm in your faith, you will not stand at all." This is the context in which Isaiah then instructed Ahaz to "ask God for a sign". By choosing not to ask for a sign Ahaz was, for all intents and purposes, unwilling to seek God's direction and was declining to commit himself to God, either personally or on behalf of his people. Isaiah was angry.

A sign will be given by God, he announced. This will be in the birth of a child. The child will be named by the mother, 'Immanuel'. This immediately reminds us of Luke 1.31 where Mary is instructed by God's messenger, the angel, to name her child 'Jesus'. All this is significant because it is the women in both passages here, and not the men, who are given authority to name the child.

Meantime, whilst Ahaz will have little that is good coming his way, the child 'Immanuel' will be eating curds and honey. This will be pleasing food for the child that is God's sign and it will be his comfort at that time when he will know to choose that which is right, and to reject that which is wrong. An aged Church of Scotland minister, in my hometown of St Andrews, put the same thought in classically elegant Scots prose during prayers in a televised service of worship, "Teach us to shun all things tawdry." By so doing we will have enacted God's will and chosen that which is God's desire. The same thought is also given in Deuteronomy 30.19 when we are directed to 'choose life':

> This day I call heaven and earth as witnesses against you that I have set before you life and death, blessings and curses. Now choose life, so that you and your children may live and that you may love the Lord your God, listen to his voice, and hold fast to him. For the Lord is your life, and he will give you many years in the land he swore to give to your fathers, Abraham, Isaac and Jacob.

'Choosing life' may not be easy. A friend of our family suffered grievously at her work, successively in two Christian organisations, for standing up to wrongdoing in each. By 'choosing life' – namely choosing that which was right and was of God – she exposed the failure of those who should have done as she did, but who did not. As a consequence, she suffered in her professional life markedly as each organisation, in turn, removed her from her position. The light of God she held before them was too bright for them to bear.

Despite much inner turmoil she knew what she had said and done was of God and that, whatever future would unfold for her, she could have done no other. In her case, 'choosing life' didn't make for an easy life. But it gave her the right life before God and within herself.

PART ONE

Is Isaiah speaking a prophetic word to you, to our world?

Suggestion for sixty seconds of reflection:

Choose a single phrase from the above passage and repeat it over and over again in your mind for sixty seconds. Or: Sit in silence or quiet for sixty seconds and reflect upon what you have read in the bible passage.

Close in prayer:

May God give you the grace not to sell yourself short, grace to risk something big for something good, grace to remember that the world is now too dangerous for anything but truth, and too small for anything but love. Amen.[26]

---

26 A benediction widely attributed to the Revd William Sloan Coffin. This is cited many times on different web platforms. "One of the clergy at the church I served in in New Jersey, the Rev Mary Frances Schjonberg, would often use it as part of a blessing she would offer at the end of a service." (D.S.)

Monday – Fourth Week

Today's Scripture reading: Haggai 1.1-15

1 [1] In the second year of King Darius, in the sixth month, on the first day of the month, the word of the Lord came by the prophet Haggai to Zerubbabel son of Shealtiel, governor of Judah, and to Joshua son of Jehozadak, the high priest: [2] Thus says the Lord of hosts: These people say the time has not yet come to rebuild the Lord's house. [3] Then the word of the Lord came by the prophet Haggai, saying: [4] Is it a time for you yourselves to live in your panelled houses, while this house lies in ruins? [5] Now therefore, thus says the Lord of hosts: Consider how you have fared. [6] You have sown much, and harvested little; you eat, but you never have enough; you drink, but you never have your fill; you clothe yourselves, but no one is warm; and you that earn wages earn wages to put them into a bag with holes.

[7] Thus says the Lord of hosts: Consider how you have fared. [8] Go up to the hills and bring wood and build the house, so that I may take pleasure in it and be honoured, says the Lord. [9] You have looked for much, and, lo, it came to little; and when you brought it home, I blew it away. Why? says the Lord of hosts. Because my house lies in ruins, while all of you hurry off to your own houses. [10] Therefore the heavens above you have withheld the dew, and the earth has withheld its produce. [11] And I have called for a drought on the land and the hills, on the grain, the new wine, the oil, on what the soil produces, on human beings and animals, and on all their labours.

[12] Then Zerubbabel son of Shealtiel, and Joshua son of Jehozadak, the high priest, with all the remnant of the people, obeyed the voice of the Lord their God, and the words of the prophet Haggai, as the Lord their God had sent him; and the people feared the Lord. [13] Then Haggai, the messenger of the Lord, spoke to the people with the Lord's message, saying, I am with you, says the Lord. [14] And the Lord stirred up the spirit of Zerubbabel son of Shealtiel, governor of Judah, and the spirit of Joshua son of Jehozadak, the high priest, and the spirit of all the remnant of the people; and they came and worked on the house of the Lord of hosts, their God, [15] on the twenty-fourth day of the month, in the sixth month.

PART ONE

Digging deeper into the prophetic voice of our ancestor Haggai:

The opening verse of Haggai Chapter One tell us when the Book of Haggai first appeared. Scholars have straightforwardly worked out that it was 520BCE. The references to Joshua, as high priest, and Zerubbabel, the governor, tell us also that Haggai was giving his prophecy about the same time or thereabouts as Zechariah.

Like Zechariah he was anxious that the Temple in Jerusalem should be rebuilt. At worship, when in exile, the people would have turned themselves to face towards Jerusalem's Temple. It was the place where true worship should be offered. Now back in Jerusalem they would be devastated that the Temple, and the city around it, was in ruins. Rebuilding had initially begun. Then, clearly anxious about their own circumstances, the people moved from rebuilding the Temple to construction of their own houses.

Haggai, conscious that return to Jerusalem required the reconstruction of the Temple if the people were to prosper, charged them with the task of completing it, "Is it a time for you . . . to live in your paneled houses, while this house lies in ruins?" he rhetorically asks. The Temple would be, as one writer has put it, ". . . part of the economic, political and legal life of the nation . . ." as well as, of course, the centre of its all-encompassing religious significance for the people.[27]

Much of the background to the rebuilding of the Temple can be found in the Book of Ezra and whilst it might be instructive to look at that, doing so would take us beyond the boundaries of this Reading Companion.

The point for us in this story comes both by reminder and encouragement. The Book of Amos gave us warnings about complacency in faith; Zechariah reassured us that in faith God's people had returned to Him; now Haggai is warning about renewed complacency and self-serving – even in the face of threats from surrounding enemies. Verses 12-15 document the willing response of Zerubbabel the governor, Joshua the High Priest and the people to Haggai's message.

His message was: 'rebuild the Temple – it is crucial to your life'. His message to us is, and now drawing on Paul's teaching in his First Letter to

---

27 Carol L. Meyers and Eric M. Meyers, *The Anchor Bible: Haggai, Zechariah 1 – 8,* Doubleday, New York, 1987, 21, 37.

the Corinthians, "We are each a Temple of God's Holy Spirit." This personal Temple, that is each one of us, must not be ignored or left unattended. It must always be developed and continually be rebuilt. In the context of our lives being lived in faith it is crucial.

Is Haggai speaking a prophetic word to you, to our world?

Suggestion for sixty seconds of reflection: Choose a single phrase from the above passage and repeat it over and over again in your mind for sixty seconds. Or: Sit in silence or quiet for sixty seconds and reflect upon what you have read in the bible passage.

Close in prayer. Perhaps using the following prayer attributed to St. Teresa of Avila . . .

> Let nothing disturb you,
> Let nothing frighten you,
> All things are passing away:
> God never changes.
> Patience obtains all things,
> Whoever has God lacks nothing;
> God alone suffices. Amen.[28]

---

28 Prayer of St Teresa of Avila. Freely available in published form and online.

Part One

Tuesday – Fourth Week

Today's Scripture reading: Haggai 2.1-9

2 In the second year of King Darius, ¹ in the seventh month, on the twenty-first day of the month, the word of the Lord came by the prophet Haggai, saying: ² Speak now to Zerubbabel son of Shealtiel, governor of Judah, and to Joshua son of Jehozadak, the high priest, and to the remnant of the people, and say, ³ Who is left among you that saw this house in its former glory? How does it look to you now? Is it not in your sight as nothing? ⁴ Yet now take courage, O Zerubbabel, says the Lord; take courage, O Joshua, son of Jehozadak, the high priest; take courage, all you people of the land, says the Lord; work, for I am with you, says the Lord of hosts, ⁵ according to the promise that I made you when you came out of Egypt. My spirit abides among you; do not fear.

⁶ For thus says the Lord of hosts: Once again, in a little while, I will shake the heavens and the earth and the sea and the dry land; ⁷ and I will shake all the nations, so that the treasure of all nations shall come, and I will fill this house with splendour, says the Lord of hosts. ⁸ The silver is mine, and the gold is mine, says the Lord of hosts. ⁹ The latter splendour of this house shall be greater than the former, says the Lord of hosts; and in this place I will give prosperity, says the Lord of hosts.

Digging deeper into the prophetic voice of our ancestor Haggai:

The two key words in this passage are 'take courage'. Through Haggai the prophet God says that the unadorned Temple which the people are rebuilding should not be compared to the grand, ornate one that Solomon had built but which was then pulled down. He asks (verse 3), "Who is left among you that saw this house in its former glory?" The present one "looks as nothing".

That does not trouble God. His concern is to encourage the people in their reconstruction work; "take courage" it says three times in verse 4. God assures his people that He is "with them" as they do their rebuilding.

It is all too easy for churches, particularly small ones, to look with envy on the larger churches and feel they cannot rise to the challenge they feel God asks of them. Nor should churches compare themselves with what they are now with what might seem to have been a more wonderful past.

When once in my former diocese a particular small church had suffered seriously through the wickedly bad actions of some of its members it was reduced to two members, a husband and wife. At the beginning of the north of Scotland's winter, when all this came about, I asked these two simply to turn up to their church each Sunday and say morning prayer together at the given time for a service. Their dedication led to others coming along. A retired priest came to the area and volunteered to minister in that small congregation. There was also a full refurbishment of the church from end to end and roof to floor. The congregation, some eight years later, remains small but is in good heart and has grown. When things could have ended, those two people 'took courage' for they knew God was with them. They did not look to the past nor yet compare what they then had with better years a long time before. They looked forward and rebuilt everything forward.

And the same applies to each of us individually. When things look grim, or not as good as they once were, or not as favourable for us as it seems to be for others, the prophet Haggai voices God's word to each of us, "take courage … for [God] is with us". God's glory will fill us just as it filled Solomon's Temple of old and as it would in the future, even if differently.

Is Haggai speaking a prophetic word to you, to our world?

Suggestion for sixty seconds of reflection: Choose a single phrase from the above passage and repeat it over and over again in your mind for sixty seconds. Or: Sit in silence or quiet for sixty seconds and reflect upon what you have read in the bible passage.

Perhaps use the following, taken from the poem 'Passage to India' by Walt Whitman *(1819-92)* as a prayer for courage and perseverance in facing present and further challengers …

Away O Soul! hoist instantly
   the anchor!
Cut the hawsers – haul out –
   shake out every sail!

Sail forth – steer for the deep
   waters only,
Reckless O soul, exploring, I
   with thee, and thou with
   me,
For we are bound where mariner
   has not yet dared
   to go,
And we will risk the ship,
   ourselves and all.

O my brave Soul!
O farther, farther sail!
O daring joy, but safe! are they
   not all the seas of God?
O farther, farther, farther sail![29]

---

29 Walt Whitman *(1819-92)* Extracts taken from Whitman's epic poem, 'Passage to India', #9. (Freely available online and in the public domain)

Wednesday – Fourth Week

Today's Scripture reading: Zephaniah 3.1-14

3¹ Ah, soiled, defiled,
  oppressing city!
² It has listened to no voice;
  it has accepted no correction.
It has not trusted in the Lord;
  it has not drawn near to its God.
³ The officials within it
  are roaring lions;
its judges are evening wolves
  that leave nothing until the morning.
⁴ Its prophets are reckless,
  faithless persons;
its priests have profaned what is sacred,
  they have done violence to the law.
⁵ The Lord within it is righteous;
  he does no wrong.
Every morning he renders his judgement,
  each dawn without fail;
  but the unjust knows no shame.
⁶ I have cut off nations;
  their battlements are in ruins;
I have laid waste their streets
  so that no one walks in them;
their cities have been made desolate,
  without people, without inhabitants.
⁷ I said, 'Surely the city[a] will fear me,
  it will accept correction;
it will not lose sight[b]
  of all that I have brought upon it.'
But they were the more eager
  to make all their deeds corrupt.

⁸ Therefore wait for me, says the Lord,
   for the day when I arise as a witness.
For my decision is to gather nations,
   to assemble kingdoms,
to pour out upon them my indignation,
   all the heat of my anger;
for in the fire of my passion
   all the earth shall be consumed.
⁹ At that time I will change the speech of the peoples
   to a pure speech,
that all of them may call on the name of the Lord
   and serve him with one accord.
¹⁰ From beyond the rivers of Ethiopia
   my suppliants, my scattered ones,
   shall bring my offering.
¹¹ On that day you shall not be put to shame
   because of all the deeds by which you have rebelled against me;
for then I will remove from your midst
   your proudly exultant ones,
and you shall no longer be haughty
   in my holy mountain.
¹² For I will leave in the midst of you
   a people humble and lowly.
They shall seek refuge in the name of the Lord –
¹³ the remnant of Israel;
they shall do no wrong
   and utter no lies,
nor shall a deceitful tongue
   be found in their mouths.
Then they will pasture and lie down,
   and no one shall make them afraid.
¹⁴ Sing aloud, O daughter Zion;
   shout, O Israel!
Rejoice and exult with all your heart,
   O daughter Jerusalem!

Digging deeper into the prophetic voice of our ancestor Zephaniah:

As we followed Amos and on to Zechariah and Haggai so we moved forwards in time and events in sequence. With Zephaniah today, we move into the period between about 640BCE to about 620BCE or thereabouts. As Amos directed the word of God's judgment against the northern kingdom of Israel so now we find Zephaniah doing the same to the southern kingdom of Judah.

Zephaniah wrote most likely early in the reign of King Josiah in the southern kingdom. Josiah had come to the throne at the age of eight and began *moral reform* from about the age of eighteen. Previous kings had not been good, "filling the land with violence and immorality".[30] Josiah began *religious reforms* when he was about twenty and during these reforms the book of the Law (the books of Genesis to Deuteronomy) was rediscovered (see 2 Kings 22.1-7 and 2 Chronicles 34.2, 8). This led to a re-doubling of Josiah's reforming enthusiasm no doubt spurred on by the warning prophecies of Zephaniah.

It is always the case, to my mind at least, that in any situation where leadership is corrupt or corrupted its pervasive and pernicious effect spreads outwards and downwards. It requires bravely courageous individuals and groups of like-minded concerned people to turn things around. Zephaniah was one such brave person. In this passage he mostly castigates the wrongdoing and the wrongdoers. But in verses 12 through 14 he foresees God leaving unchallenged, ". . . a people humbly and lowly . . . seek[ing] refuge in the name of the Lord . . . they shall do no wrong and utter no lies . . ." Their well-being and their future will be safe and secure. On this basis they can rejoice and praise God. This is the message of hope Zephaniah offers to those who shun wickedness and make faithful obedience to God their realized desire.

---

30 Augustin Gnanachezhian, *South Asia Bible Commentary*, 1181.

PART ONE

Is Zephaniah speaking a prophetic word to you, to our world?

Suggestion for sixty seconds of reflection: Choose a single phrase from the above passage and repeat it over and over again in your mind for sixty seconds. Or: Sit in silence or quiet for sixty seconds and reflect upon what you have read in the bible passage.

"Stay humble and pray" is a motto frequently seen printed on clothes and bumper stickers in the USA. Is it to remind the person who bears it or is it borne to influence others? Maybe both? As our communities, and not least our churches move into new chapters of post-pandemic life, we need to find ways of coming back together. It is only natural that as we grow into God's mission for us, we will need to have "plenty forgiveness and no talk stink", to quote a well-known Hawai'ian motto. Humility and prayer are vital for a spiritually healthy Christian community. As we pray for ourselves pray also for those around and near to you. Kupuna Maunakea wrote the following prayer . . . it is correctly given here for, even though originally published in the USA, it contains the English spelling of 'Saviour':

> We give thanks for Your grace,
> And Your great love.
> Our Heavenly Father,
> We seek Your blessings.
> Guide us in our leadership
> As we go forward.
> Lead us with wisdom and
> Understanding in our projects.
> We thank you again
> Our Lord and Saviour.
> Amen.[31]

---

31 Kupuna Katherine Kamalukukui Maunakea, 'A Prayer for Leadership', in *Kupuna Maunakea's Book of Prayers*, 4th Edition, 10, © The Katherine K. Maunakea Foundation, 1994, Nanakuli, Hawai'i.

Thursday – Fourth Week

Today's Scripture reading: Zephaniah 3.15-20

3 ¹⁵ The Lord has taken away the judgements against you,
    he has turned away your enemies.
The king of Israel, the Lord, is in your midst;
    you shall fear disaster no more.
¹⁶ On that day it shall be said to Jerusalem:
Do not fear, O Zion;
    do not let your hands grow weak.
¹⁷ The Lord, your God, is in your midst,
    a warrior who gives victory;
he will rejoice over you with gladness,
    he will renew you in his love;
he will exult over you with loud singing
¹⁸   as on a day of festival.
I will remove disaster from you,
    so that you will not bear reproach for it.
¹⁹ I will deal with all your oppressors
    at that time.
And I will save the lame
    and gather the outcast,
and I will change their shame into praise
    and renown in all the earth.
²⁰ At that time I will bring you home,
    at the time when I gather you;
for I will make you renowned and praised
    among all the peoples of the earth,
when I restore your fortunes
    before your eyes, says the Lord.

Digging deeper into the prophetic voice of our ancestor Zephaniah:

These verses are beautiful. As we near the end of Advent so now we find what it will be like when God rules amongst us. God "will rejoice over [his people] with gladness . . . and renew [his people] in his love."

This is the 'promised dawn' that I have used as the title of this Advent program. This is what God hopes for His people. And it is the hope of God's people. Each strives to make it real.

Is Zephaniah speaking a prophetic word to you, to our world?

Suggestion for sixty seconds of reflection: Choose a single phrase from the above passage and repeat it over and over again in your mind for sixty seconds. Or: Sit in silence or quiet for sixty seconds and reflect upon what you have read in the bible passage.

Close in prayer ...

God the Father's love for us is revealed in the coming of Jesus our saviour. In trust we place our petitions before him: (add your prayers for our world, your family and friends, yourself). Like Mary and Joseph we long for the coming of your Son into our lives. Hear our prayers as we wait to celebrate the birth of your Jesus. We ask this through Christ our Lord. Amen.[32]

---

32 Desmond Knowles, *Voicing A Thought On Sunday, Homilies and Prayers of the Faithful for the Three-Year Cycle,* The Columbia Press, Blackrock, Co Dublin, Ireland, 1992, 17, (adapted D.S.).

Friday – Fourth Week

Today's Scripture reading: Malachi 3.1-4

3¹ See, I am sending my messenger to prepare the way before me, and the Lord whom you seek will suddenly come to his temple. The messenger of the covenant in whom you delight – indeed, he is coming, says the Lord of hosts. ² But who can endure the day of his coming, and who can stand when he appears?

For he is like a refiner's fire and like fullers' soap; ³ he will sit as a refiner and purifier of silver, and he will purify the descendants of Levi and refine them like gold and silver, until they present offerings to the Lord in righteousness. ⁴ Then the offering of Judah and Jerusalem will be pleasing to the Lord as in the days of old and as in former years.

Digging deeper into the prophetic voice of our ancestor Malachi:

It is very likely that maybe as much as four hundred years have elapsed since Amos' preaching and this book of dialogues between Malachi (literally 'The Messenger') and God. From our readings in Haggai we know the Jerusalem Temple had been rebuilt and the people had been encouraged in its rebuilding for 'God was with them'.

Sadly however, things had slipped after the first enthusiasm of disciplined and energetic rebuilding had waned. So here we have a prophet announcing that God himself will come to his Temple and will cleanse it once and for all. As silver is refined and as fullers' soap cleans so God will come and will do the same for his Temple.

Each of us individually and all of us together are God's Temple now. Where we have fallen or been brought down by others, whether deliberately or unknowingly, God will come to us and before Him we will stand. The question is, "who can endure the day of his coming?" and "who will stand when He appears."

Confessing our sin and admitting our failure, together with assurance of God's forgiveness of the genuinely repentant will be the way we can stand and face God and thus be accepted into His arms . . . forever blessed.

The composer, Handel, framed words from this reading into his evocatively moving *'Who may abide the day of his coming'* in his wonderful oratorio, the Messiah.

PART ONE

Is Malachi speaking a prophetic word to you, to our world?

Suggestion for sixty seconds of reflection: Choose a single phrase from the above passage and repeat it over and over again in your mind for sixty seconds. Or: Sit in silence or quiet for sixty seconds and reflect upon what you have read in the bible passage.

Many churches often sing the old Gospel hymn, 'Standing in the need of prayer'. The final line always rings true, "It's me, it's me, it's me O Lord, standing in the need of prayer." This is, I believe, true for all of us. In what ways are we in need of healing from brokenness caused by sin? Close in prayer . . .

>Wonderful Counsellor,
>be with me as I reflect on all that has happened today:
>what I did . . .
>why I did it . . .
>what I have learned . . .
>what I have given to others . . .
>what others have given to me . . .
>how I have shown my faith . . .
>how I have shared my faith . . .
>how I have honoured your name . . .
>what I will take into tomorrow . . .
>what I will leave with you, Lord.
>Thank you.
>Amen.[33]

---

33 Rupert Bristow, *Only Connect*, 13.

Saturday – Fourth Week

Today's Scripture reading: Micah 5.2-5a

² But you, O Bethlehem of Ephrathah,
    who are one of the little clans of Judah,
from you shall come forth for me
    one who is to rule in Israel,
whose origin is from of old,
    from ancient days.
³ Therefore he shall give them up until the time
    when she who is in labour has brought forth;
then the rest of his kindred shall return
    to the people of Israel.
⁴ And he shall stand and feed his flock in the strength of the Lord,
    in the majesty of the name of the Lord his God.
And they shall live secure, for now he shall be great
    to the ends of the earth;
⁵ and he shall be the one of peace.
    If the Assyrians come into our land
    and tread upon our soil,
we will raise against them seven shepherds
    and eight installed as rulers.

Digging deeper into the prophetic voice of our ancestor Micah:

We are now, in this final reading for Advent, back to the last twenty-five years of the eighth century BCE. Micah is therefore one of our readings from an early period of Hebrew history. Often regarded as the 'prophet of and for the poor' he also summarizes the hope for a future messiah to restore everything his people long for. He shared the view that God would use surrounding enemies to punish the faithlessness of the northern kingdom, Israel. This would serve as a warning to those of the southern kingdom, Judah.

Micah's warning of judgment is to those who seek to undermine true worship whether for purposes of self-seeking or self-advancement or through political caprice. And, in contrast with this, he speaks of the hope of salvation to those who remain faithful. In his commentary notes Blessen Matthew Sam says that Micah, "speaks of the coming of the Messiah and of the eventual restoration of true worship in a restored Jerusalem". [34]

In our day, and within the Christian framework, we are the New Jerusalem. When Christ returns in his second coming God's fulfilment of all things will be complete.

At this Christmas time we remember with thanksgiving his first coming and with eagerness share the prophetic hope of him coming again.

Is Micah speaking a prophetic word to you, to our world?

Suggestion: For sixty seconds simply reflect on the coming of Jesus into your own life. And be prepared to speak of this to others quietly and discreetly.

Close with this prayer by Karl Rahner, S.J., entitled 'I Am There' . . .

> Now God says to us
>
> what He has already said to the earth as a whole
> through His grace-filled birth:
>
> I am there. I am with you.
> I am your life. I am your time.
> I am the gloom of your daily routine. Why will you not hear it?
> I weep your tears – pour yours out to me.
> I am your joy.
> Do not be afraid to be happy; ever since I wept, joy is the standard of living that is really more suitable than the anxiety and grief of those who have no hope.

---

34 Blessen Matthew Sam, 'Micah', *South Asia Bible Commentary*, 1161.

The Promised Dawn

I am the blind alley of all your paths,
For when you no longer know how to go any farther,
Then you have reached me,
Though you are not aware of it.

I am in your anxiety, for I have shared it.
I am in the prison of your finiteness,
For my love has made me your prisoner.

I am in your death,
For today I began to die with you, because I was born,
And I have not let myself be spared any real part of this experience.

I am present in your needs;
I have suffered them and they are now transformed.

I am there.
I no longer go away from this world.
Even if you do not see me now, I am there.

My love is unconquerable.
I am there.
It is Christmas.
Light the Candles! They have more right to exist then all the darkness.
It is Christmas.
Christmas that lasts forever.
Amen.[35]

---

35 Karl Rahner, 'I Am There' in *The Great Church Year: The Best of Karl Rahner's Homilies, Sermons and Meditations*, Herder & Herder, 1994, Freiburg im Breisgau. First published in, Karl Rahner, *The Eternal Year*, Helicon Press Inc, 1st edn, 1964. Widely available online. The 'Amen' has been added (D.S.).

PART TWO

Background material to each of our ancestors,
those prophets in the Old Testament from whom we read
in this Advent Reading Companion

In the pages that follow you will find detailed background material that is supplementary to those Bible passages which form the daily devotional reading in Part One of this book.

ISAIAH

In the devotional section of this book, Part One, are four readings from Isaiah. These are Sunday Old Testament readings set in the internationally adopted *Revised Common Lectionary* for Year A of the three year cycle of Bible readings for use at communion services.

What follows in this section of Part Two are general, and largely non-technical, background notes. These are designed to give supplementary information about the Book of the Prophet Isaiah. In addition it is hoped that they will give further resources for deeper reflection upon the context in which Isaiah wrote.

Who was Isaiah?

By asking, and then seeking, an answer to this seemingly simple question we become part of a movement of intense interest in the historical study of the Bible. In part, as we shall see, this movement was encouraged by increasingly skilful archaeological investigation of middle and near eastern sites. What was found during those investigations yielded invaluable insight into those cultures whose structures and artefacts are increasingly being unearthed. Insights into daily life have been gleaned. New discoveries are made yielding us further knowledge of how our ancestors lived in the times of the prophets of the Old Testament. Sites of ritual activity have been found which, in turn, have offered clues to practices and habits associated with religious observation.

Likewise, discoveries have been made which reinforced, or corrected, previous intuitions that had been thought for a very long time from previously known or discovered ancient documents.

One such was the discovery at Qumran, on the Dead Sea margin, of a scroll of the Book of Isaiah dating from the period just shortly before the Common Era (CE), previously and traditionally given as 'In the Year of Our Lord' (*Anno Domini*, AD). Hitherto, the earliest known scroll of the Book of Isaiah dated from the ninth century. Remarkably, but perhaps not unsurprisingly, barely any linguistic differences exist between the two documents. What we previously had, dating from the ninth century CE, is now vouched as accurate by the careful discovery and recovery of the same

PART TWO

text, but dated over nine hundred years earlier. In turn, it will have derived from previously existing scrolls circulating at that time.

Therefore, what we have learned about Isaiah, referring both to the text that bears his name and who he was as author, has significant linguistic, historical and textual provenance.

The earliest Christian writers, obviously much closer in time to the life of Jesus than we are now, could look at those texts which we know as the Old Testament and find passages which anticipated the coming of Jesus as God's messiah. For example, St Jerome, translator of the Bible into Latin, writing in Bethlehem in the late fourth century and early fifth century CE, spoke of Isaiah, his ancestor in the faith, very much as a later Christian evangelist might have been described. Jerome said:

> Isaiah is an evangelist and apostle, not only a prophet . . . This book of the Bible contains all the mysteries of the Lord and proclaims him as Emmanuel born of a virgin, as a worker of glorious deeds and signs, as having died and been buried and rising from hell, and, indeed, as the Savior of all the nations.[1]

This, then, is a simple though profound insight into how early Christian writers might view their ancestors the prophets. Very occasionally we find the same today. Thus, in writing to a friend about my experience of delivering the Advent Program to the three congregations in Hawai'i which had invited me to do so in Advent 2022, I spoke of the profound impact it was having upon me. Here is what I wrote first:

> What has been a particular learning for me is the fact that in relation to the prophets of the Old Testament [the Hawai'ians] speak of them as their ancestors. We might prefer the term 'forebears' or 'forefathers' but the use of the term 'ancestors' signifies a deep cultural link between who the Hawai'ians are now and their 'ancestors' in the prophets of the Old Testament. It all makes for a profoundly different way of reading the scriptures.

---

1   From 'Prologue' to the *Commentary on Isaiah*, 'Corpus Christianorum: Series latina; 73:1', cited from Robert Louis Wilken, xiii, *Isaiah: Interpreted by Early Christian and Medieval Commentators*, trans. and ed. by Robert Louis Wilken with Angela Russell Christman and Michael J. Hollerich, William B. Erdmans Publishing Company, Grand Rapids, Michigan, 2007.

And my friend replied:

> The wonderful insight of the Hawai'ian Christians, concerning their perceived ancestral relationship with the Old Testament prophets, has provided a flash of light for me that brings into focus the oneness, and timeless spiritual continuity of God's human family in Christ.
>
> I wonder why I did not see this for myself – those messengers of God are no longer ancient, remote believers from a different race, and from a different place. This revelation has brought them as close to me as my own grandfather; the testaments merge, the covenants merge, and the whole is larded, so to speak, with a continuous family thread of witnesses, all with a common family identity and likeness.[2]

So, and to summarise thus far, when we seek to identify who Isaiah was we find first of all that he is someone who is one of our ancestors. Someone who, like the other Old Testament prophets we shall shortly be considering, is in direct continuity with us. And like St Jerome the Bible translator we shall see in these prophets vital words that link with Christian testimony to the coming of Jesus Christ. Hugh of St Victor (1096 – 1141CE) tellingly summarised this:

> All of Divine Scripture is one book, and that one book is Christ, because all of Divine Scripture speaks of Christ, and all of Divine Scripture is fulfilled in Christ.[3]

With equal direction we shall find ourselves tested and challenged by some of the observations each of our ancestors, the prophets, had with respect to human failing.

The opening verse of Isaiah tells us when he was alive, "The vision of Isaiah son of Amoz,[4] which he saw concerning Judah and Jerusalem in the days of Uzziah, Jotham, Ahaz, and Hezekiah, kings of Judah." This litany of names, perhaps seemingly innocuous to the untrained eye, is nevertheless important. It places Isaiah and his prophetic utterances in a

---

2   Private email correspondence with John Louch, Orkney, Scotland, December 5th and 8th 2022, quoted with permission. This correspondence is deliberately duplicated from Part 1 due to the importance of what John Louch wrote.

3   Hugh of St Victor, *De arca Noe morali 2.7,* Patrologiae cursus completes, Series latina 176:642c-d, cited from Wilken, *op cit,* xv.

4   The 'Amoz' mentioned here is not the same person as the prophet Amos.

Part Two

substantial period of the eighth century BCE (i.e. 'Before Common Era', and 'Before Christ', BC). The siege assault against Jerusalem took place in 701BCE during the reign of Hezekiah and is referred to in Isaiah 36 – 37 with Isaiah foretelling the safety of Jerusalem. On the basis of this evidence, and there is no reason to doubt this ancient historical source any more than any other attested literary document, we can locate Isaiah the man, our ancestor, within, or even to, the forty-year period 740 – 700BCE approximately. The written corpus of his prophetic ministry is to be found in Chapters 1 – 39 of the Book of Isaiah. Different authorship applies from Chapter 40 onwards to the end of the Book.

With those details noted we should be wary of assuming that Isaiah was the exact, or single, author of the book that bears his name. Chapters 36 – 39, for example are likewise found in 2 Kings 18.13 – 20.19. They are also found partially paralleled in 2 Chronicles 32. This should not disturb any recognition of the authenticity of Isaiah and of the times in which he lived. Multiple attestation adds to the veracity of the historical record. Also, and simply to note in passing, that Isaiah Chapters 24 – 27 appear to reflect a particular type of mythology rather than historical narrative. More of that to follow.

Unsurprisingly, the Book of Isaiah says very little about the man whose name the book bears. We have already noted a forty-year span in which he was active. Nonetheless the reference at 8.3-4 to him going "to the prophetess" and then her conceiving and bearing him a son refers to conjugal relations between Isaiah and his wife. Verse 18 speaks of more children than this one. Identifying them this way suggests they are amongst those who would, if occasion demanded, vouch for what their father said within his prophetic ministry to those around them.

In beautifully picturesque imagery in Chapter Six Isaiah speaks of his call to speak God's words. Even though he was a 'man of unclean lips' nonetheless the cleansing of those lips through God's cauterising action occasioned him the authority to do what God required him to do. And yet, as Chapter Six progresses we find Isaiah to be a lone voice in a desert where no ears could hear the importance that he was called to voice. The outcome of all his prophetic warning would be a simple stump of new growth, tiny, yet durable and likely to germinate and grow.

Fundamental in realising who Isaiah was, however, is acknowledging that his concern was not with himself. Isaiah could not entertain any twenty-first century 'celebrity culture'. No; Isaiah's concern was the wrong that comes when one person sins against another and when individuals and communities sin against God. This latter includes worship of other gods as well as empty, show-case, devotion to the God of the Hebrews devoid of commitment. In our day we could, and should, add sins against the environment – God's creation.

How the Book of Isaiah is structured

Basically it is in three parts; each distinguished from the others by the likely dates of their authorship. Isaiah 1 – 39 comes from the last forty years or so of the eighth century, as we have already noted. The other two sections, though often considered as one, are Chapters 40 – 55 and 56 – 66. The former of these would appear to be set against the period of the exile of the Hebrew people in Babylon and the latter of their return to Palestine and issues that then faced them.

As our four devotional passages from Isaiah are taken from within Isaiah 1 – 39 it is to this which I shall now restrict myself:

Chapters 1 – 5 are orientated towards the Hebrew people.
Chapters 6 – 11 would appear to reflect the Syro-Ephraimite war.
Chapters 13 – 23 speak against warlike surrounding nations.
Chapters 28 – 33 have warnings on the revolt against Sennacherib.

We have already spoken of Chapters 36 - 39 to be found duplicated in 2 Kings 18.13 – 20.19. Chapters 34 – 35 more appropriately reflect the style and content of Isaiah 40 and onwards. The highly mythological features of Chapters 24 – 27 seem not to reflect any particular historical episode to which Isaiah may be attached. Likely dating of this section could be around the early part of the sixth century BCE and therefore outwith our dating of the activity in the Book of Isaiah to be from 740 – 700BCE.

Christopher Seitz supports the metaphor of 'an orchestral score' to portray the complexity that is the Book of Isaiah recognising, that if so, it is "a piece of music with quite a few composers".[5] As such this is an appealing metaphor for Chapter One of Isaiah functions very adequately as an 'overture' to the whole work with an emphasis of the failures, and thus the future, of Jerusalem.

---

5 Christopher Seitz, *Isaiah 1 – 39,* John Knox Press, Louisville, 1993, 10.

Textually, we note that the first verse of Isaiah could only have been written *after* the composition of the book as a whole for until the lifespan of its authorship was completed it would not have been known within whose reigns to place it.

In summary then we recognise Isaiah to have a complex structure reflecting the work of several authors each of whom had a uniting concern that reflected Israel and Judah's failures before God and of its fate before surrounding empires bent on its conquest. If the nation does not repent then God's anger against the people of the Hebrews will be meted out by those nations when they overcome its defences.

Historical Context

At the time of Isaiah's composition in the eighth century BCE Assyria, to north and to which King Ahaz of Judah had to pay heavy duties, was a superpower, albeit one under threat itself from the Babylonians. Egypt, to the south of Judah, was stirring rebellion in the hearts of those vassal nations under the control of Assyria with a view to subduing them under its control. Judah was very much at the epicentre of this turbulence.

King Ahaz of Judah sought alliance with Assyria, effectively against the kings of Israel and Syria around 735BCE. This was against prophetic counsel as recorded in Isaiah 7.1-25 (verses 3ff especially) not to make foreign alliances. The inevitable result was that Judah was indebted to Assyria. Sections of Isaiah 1 – 35 variously reflect this period, even if not in the strict chronological sequence that we, in our day, would expect of historical and narrative documentation.

Rebellion against Assyria by King Ahaz' son, Hezekiah, brought about invasion of Judah and the destruction of many of its cities with Jerusalem being miraculously spared (Isaiah 36-39).

How sadly familiar all of this is. In February 2022 immense Russian forces invaded Ukraine, following on from previous incursions into Crimea and other Ukranian territories. As of now Europe is at war. Moldova fears for its future. Ukraine is allied with western nations for military hardware and combat training. The Russian Orthodox Church leadership is aligned with the 'Greater Russian' ambitions of Vladimir Putin. Whilst we in the west deplore Russia's wrongdoing in this conflict we must not forget mistakes we have made in the invasion of other countries; Iraq in 2003 is one such cause for lament.

Is it too simplistic or naive, or, alternatively, might it just be apposite once again to hear Isaiah's warning not to turn to the dominions of the earth but rather to hear the voice of God and in God to put our trust?

Geographical Context

Then, as now, Israel-Palestine has been at the confluence and is the epicentre of conflicting forces, most of which over the centuries have proved unreconcilable. Presenting a map of where the two kingdoms were might, in an ideal world, give a snapshot of how each existed in the eastern Mediterranean. But even that would be only a partial glimpse of the reality for no map can entirely present the exact picture. Ancient geopolitical and economic alliances defy cartography. Military alliances at the time varied and shifted as polity and circumstance dictated. Likewise borders moved and interpretation of their locations will inevitably vary from scholar to scholar as map-making at that time did not exist.

Broadly speaking however, the Northern Kingdom, largely made up of the majority of tribes which rebelled against King Solomon's son, Rehoboam, occupied an area north of, and then surrounding the Sea of Galilee westwards to the Mediterranean Sea from just north of Carmel and southwards to just beyond Joppa. The border of the Northern Kingdom then followed a line, generally eastwards, just south of Jericho, around the northern edge of the Dead Sea to include the northern half of its eastern shore, and then back northerly more or less parallel to the River Jordan.

The Southern Kingdom had no Mediterranean coastline border. On the east it bordered the Dead Sea south of Jericho, round to the south shoreline of the Dead Sea and then southerly into the Negev Desert where it then traced a gentle westerly arc before returning northwards more or less along a line to the foot of the Judean mountains.

I will say more about why, or how, the two kingdoms came about in following section on the Book of the Prophet Amos.

AMOS

Not too long ago I was in conversation with an engaging lay person from South Carolina. He had served in the United States Air Force. During his professional military career he had flown bombers from an air base in Eastern England. Whilst there he was in contact with local anti-nuclear protesters contesting the presence of cruise missiles on military bases.

Rather than engage in confrontation or, equally, to ignore these people he formed the better option of getting to know them, preferably as friends rather than combatants in ideological disagreement or dispute. This he did. The outcome was that each learned more of the others' perspective from a position of personal respect rather than assumed or given hostility, at worst, or for that matter distanced objectivization.

This little vignette well serves as an introduction to the Book of Amos! Amos contains much that will disturb and challenge the modern-day reader. But rather than discount either the book itself, or fillet out from attention those bits we don't like we will do well if we get to know who Amos was, to understand why he said what he said, and thereby understand what it was, from the upcoming crisis he foresaw, that sheds light on the plight facing our world today.

Who was Amos?

Unsurprisingly perhaps, little or nothing is known about Amos' family circumstances and cross-references about him from other sources have yet to be discovered. It is likely that none exist anyway. That said, his home, Tekoa, was a military outpost / village some ten miles south west of Jerusalem and to the south of Bethlehem in the Judean hills. Second Chronicles 11.5-12 speaks of it being fortified by Rehoboam, "Rehoboam resided in Jerusalem, and he built cities for defense in Judah. He built up Bethlehem, Etam, Tekoa . . . He made the fortresses strong, and put commanders in them . . . and made them very strong".

We know also that Tekoa was rural and agricultural. The first verse of the Book of Amos speaks of him as ". . . among the shepherds of Tekoa . . ."

This could initially suggest modesty in self-description. Amos' circumstances, however, might be otherwise. The Hebrew word that describes him as a shepherd is *noqed*. The only other location where this word is found in the Old Testament is at 2 Kings 3.4 where Mesha, king of Moab, was a sheep breeder and significant supplier of sheep. By reasonable inference we may therefore suggest that Amos was not so much a lonely sheep guardian on the hillside but arguably an established and well-connected individual of some substance.

A further reference, Amos 7.14, yields more detail, "I am a herdsman, and a dresser of sycamore trees." Sycamore fig trees would not grow well on the upland slopes of the Judean hills, though would in the warmer lower altitudes closer to the Dead Sea. They required individual attention to bring them to fruit. Thus, Amos either had land, or had access to land, or at the very least was involved in work that took him across a significant tract of territory rising westward of the Dead Sea trading his products in the region and, conceivably, beyond.

From this locus, and taking him away from his duties, Amos was called by God to prophesy, "Go, prophesy to my people Israel" (7.15) and this in spite of his personal claim not to be fitted for the task, "I am no prophet, nor a prophet's son . . ." (7.14). And yet, he heard and felt a call to have to go and to prophesy and to that call he faithfully responded. Anyone who opposed him therefore opposed the will of God.

His task, as a prophet, was to follow this call and go to the northern kingdom, Israel, well away from his Judah home and address the words God would give him to the successors of those tribes whose separation from Judah saw the unity of King Solomon's reign sundered. How he was received, and with what suspicion he was viewed as his critical words were heard can be but a matter of conjecture. The task given him was neither for those of faint-hearted disposition nor for someone of tender faith. Of stern stuff Amos clearly was for the message he went north to deliver was uncompromising. It would seem that Amos had no choice but to follow the vocation that called him forward. Clearly referencing rhetorically the call that had come to him he says, "The Lord God has spoken; who can but prophesy?" (3.8b)

How the Book of Amos is structured

At one and the same time Amos, the prophet, is in the prophetic continuity of Elijah, Elisha and all those others in 1 & 2 Samuel and 1 & 2 Kings that saw the Hebrew people through their first two hundred years of monarchy and yet he is distinct from them. The early prophets secured their livelihood through their prophetic work. Amos, as we saw in the previous section, was called by God from an entirely different sphere of life and, conceivably, returned to it when his work in the northern kingdom of Israel was finished.

Unlike the early prophets whose utterances were led by means of Spirit-inspiration (1 Samuel 10-11) Amos' authority comes from the 'word' that he receives from God. How and in what form God addressed him we do not know, but we have the written testimony of Amos that God did so.

Amos spoke God's word to the people, to the kingdom of Israel to the north. In the majority of his indictments Amos names their failings, their sins against God, and follows this with a prophetic denunciation given in the name of God, "Therefore, thus says the Lord God . . ." (3.11), or "Therefore thus I will do to you, O Israel . . ." (4.12a) and so on before announcing God's proclamation and verdict against the nation and people.

What we find given is a judgment that God will end his favour towards His people. The time for repentance and turning from wrongdoing is now past. The day of social reform and reconciliation with God is long gone. A total disruption has become the only solution God will countenance. Amos, having been given this message, pronounces the most severe judgment direct from God and in God's name, "I will send a fire . . ." (1.4), "I will not revoke the punishment . . ." (2.1); "I will punish you . . ." (3.2); and chillingly, "I am raising up against you a nation . . ." (6.14); "I will kill with the sword . . ." (9.1).

Why does Amos direct all this at the people of the Hebrews? One clear reason is that they are the chosen people of God and, to put it in my words, they should have done better! Because they are so favoured they should have responded in faith to God and to one another far more assuredly than they did. God had delivered his people into a promised land. A lot is therefore expected of them, "Hear this word that the Lord has spoken against you, O people of Israel, against the whole family that I brought up out of the land of Egypt: You only have I known of all the families of the earth; *therefore I will punish you* for all your iniquities". (3.1-2, italics mine). The same message is also there at 2.10ff and 9.7-10.

God expects of his people justice and righteousness, care for the poor, faithfulness towards Him in worship and the right use of goods and wealth. Where these are absent God's faithful people have failed. There is nothing new in what Amos is saying to the people – he is reminding them of that which they have long since set aside. Amos is called by God to announce to the people that they have departed too far from that which is demanded of them by God. His words are directed against the northern kingdom, Israel. However we should not be led to think that what Amos said did not apply to the southern kingdom as well.

Over the centuries the scroll that holds the words of this book were safeguarded. Nonetheless it was added to by various editors and redactors. Amongst these is the denunciation against Judah for its transgressions as documented in 2.4-5. This is the only section in the Book of Amos that refers to sins against God to the exclusion of sins against other people. The NRSV at 2.4-5 notes that, "The language of the accusation, *law of the Lord . . . his statutes . . . after which their ancestors walked,* is that of Deuteronomy, indicating that the judgment against Judah was added after the time of Amos and probably even after Jerusalem had fallen to the Babylonians".[6]

Thus what was spoken to and against the north was deemed, by the one who penned this insertion, as applicable equally to the south. In the daily readings that form Part One of the book you are now reading I offer suggestive thoughts of the way we, especially in the UK, have dethroned God and failed in our obedience to all that He rightly expects of us. None of this is new. It is a reminder of that which always has been for the people of faith and for those who deny faith. In such circumstances God's judgment comes.

Not all the Book of Amos is prophecy. There is some hymnody albeit in fragmentary form. The passages found in 4.13, 5.8-9, and 9.5-6 are likely to have been drawn from worship settings. The first of these concludes a preceding litany of what God has done amongst the people of Israel with praise-notes of God's universal and cosmic authority. The second is similar; acknowledging God as controller of day and night, sea and rain, and asserts his power against human might as seen in lightning and storm. The third continues this theme, 'bookended' with two credal statements, "The Lord, God of hosts . . .", and ". . . the Lord is his name."

At the end of the book there is a message of hope, 9.11-15. Even if a later addition and even if the people of the Hebrews were to suffer the fate

---

6   Italics original.

which Amos foresaw nonetheless, under God's providence, "never again shall they be plucked up out of the land that I have given them . . ." for, ultimately, God saves and restores.

Amos, unlike his predecessors the prophets of earlier times who did not write, either wrote what he had proclaimed himself or another did so from the memory of what had been heard. It is equally plausible that Amos' speeches (his 'oracles') were collected together and then later edited into the collection we now have as one Old Testament book. Whatever the case, what was written, was written because it was deemed important. Later compilers of the Bible have agreed so. Perhaps by 'making friends' with Amos we can recognise this for ourselves however hard we might find accepting, or maybe recognising the significance of what he had to say and why he was called to say it even if we might demur from the actual words he used.

Historical Context

The Book of the Prophet Amos is a product of its time and place. We noted above where Isaiah fitted into the historic line of monarchs of Judah. We now find Amos appearing in the reign of Uzziah of Judah (783-742BCE)[7]. Around 757/6 Uzziah contracted leprosy with government then falling to Jotham, his son, to be co-regent. Jeroboam II was king of Israel (786-746BCE)[8]. The first verse of the Book of Amos names both monarchs, with supporting attestation in 7.9-11; the latter further affirming that Amos had travelled north to voice his prophetic utterance during the reign of Jeroboam II.

Interestingly Amos does not mention Jotham, this yielding a thought that the Book of Amos, or rather the prophetic utterances which gave rise to it, originate from between 783 to 757BCE. However, a more specific period can be considered for Amos' activity in Israel. Evidence from archaeology (Strata VI at Hazor) details a violent earthquake around 760BCE supporting the possibility that Amos began his prophetic work two years before that date. Prophesying 'two years before the earthquake' (1.1) suggests that Amos time in Israel for his prophetic ministry was no longer than that in time, and might be of shorter conceivably duration.

---

7 NRSV 2 Kings 15.1-6 (note). Uzziah was also known as Azariah.
8 NRSV 2 Kings 14.23-29 (note)

Geographical Context

I have described how the context in which Amos was active was that of two divided kingdoms. In the north, occupying most of the territory of David and Solomon's kingdom, was Israel. To the south, including Jerusalem, was the remainder - the less prosperous Judah. We need to look briefly and in summary form how this situation of the two kingdoms had come about.

So, by way of earlier historical background, and according to the biblical record, King Solomon had acceded to the throne of King David, in the previously united single kingdom that incorporated both the later areas of Israel and Judah. Solomon came to the throne around 970BCE. Up to this point, and for a time thereafter, accurate history is precarious, though by the 9th Century BCE it is certain that Solomon's kingdom had and did exist as a single unitary entity. Whatever reasons modern historians might give for the origins of the divided kingdoms, the biblical writers give a theological explanation

1 & 2 Kings documents the period from the accession of Solomon all the way through to around 560BCE but does so, not within the traditions of historical narrative as we would understand this in the 'western' post-Enlightenment framework. Rather it is a religious testimony to the faithfulness, or otherwise, of the people of the Hebrews and those who ruled them.

To begin with, the reign of Solomon was, in the one move, feted with prosperity and success. The first Temple in Jerusalem was built. Material success was marked with significant international renown and prestige as signified in the visit of the Queen of Sheba. Gold and huge wealth are documented in 1 Kings along with the fame of Solomon's desire for, and exercise of, wisdom. There was, however, a darker side to events surrounding King Solomon.

In 1 Kings 11 we find Solomon gathering wives and concubines a-plenty. They were taken from lands and nations about which, 'the Lord had said to the Israelites, "You shall not enter into marriage with them, neither shall they with you; for they will surely incline your heart to follow their gods"; Solomon clung to these in love.' In addition to his passion for women Solomon's acquisition of great wealth was also contradictory to the Hebrew Law. Deuteronomy 17 (verse 17 specifically refers both the marriage and wealth).

Solomon, contrary to God's will, followed other gods: Astarte goddess of the Sidonians and Milcom, "the abomination of the Ammonites", and likewise Chemosh of Moab. Furthermore, he worshipped before the gods of "all his foreign wives". It was because of all this that God's anger was kindled against Solomon. Divisions arising from pent-up grumblings and significant mis-leadership were never far away as Solomon's rule continued. Things were beginning to implode, so to speak.

Within a very short time after his death the northern tribes revolted and established themselves as the northern kingdom, Israel, under Jeroboam I. From an initially promising start, however, things began to fail and fall away from God's favour. Israel would suffer attack and be overthrown by its enemies and in due course its people would be removed into exile. It was to warn the people of the north that Amos came among them thus to speak God's word that their time to put things right was now past and His punishment was coming upon them. What Amos prophesied would happen did, in due course, happen.

God did for a time protect the southern kingdom, Judah, because of His favour towards the line of succession from David. God would similarly protect the Temple in Jerusalem in trust that it would continue to be a blessing to God. This favour was not to last however. Jerusalem would in time, following the fate of the larger and more prosperous and fertile northern kingdom, Israel, be lost to eventual capture with its leading citizenry also removed to foreign captivity in Babylon. Jerusalem and its Temple were sacked.

As we move now to look at the books of Zechariah and Haggai so we jump forward in history to the time when the Hebrew people are returning or rather, have returned, from exilic captivity to their home lands. Zechariah and Haggai were significantly influential in what happened as the people re-settled in their historic 'promised land'.

ZECHARIAH

Who was Zechariah?

The first verse of the Book of Zechariah speaks of him as the "son of Berechiah son of Iddo". Zechariah's task was to inspire the people, returning from exile, to rebuild both the Temple in Jerusalem and its city.

Chapters 1 – 8 of Zechariah reflect a different period, and thus different authorship, from chapters 9 – 14 of Zechariah. These latter, which to be clear are not part of our study, suggest a later period of composition with a more negative, or perhaps more pessimistic, perspective on the restoration that had by then been undertaken.

Chapters 1-8 are confidently dated in the NRSV from "October / November 520BCE".[9] Taking the chronology in the NRSV to be accurate, chapter 7.1 reads, "[in the] fourth year of King Darius the word of the Lord came to Zechariah on the fourth day of the ninth month, which is Chislev". The NRSV dates this as 518BCE. We can take this to represent the prophet's final vision and message. In effect, this amounts to a two-year period of recorded prophetic activity, namely 520BCE – 518BCE..

The name Zechariah was common at the time. The Book of Ezra at 5.1 and 6.14 names Zechariah "son of Iddo"[10] with all sources confirming that he and Haggai were conducting their prophetic ministries concurrently and in complimentary manner. The *South Asia Bible Commentary* says that Iddo, "was probably the priest who returned to Jerusalem from Babylon with Zerubbabel and Joshua (Nehemiah 12.1-4, 16). He was a prominent man at the time (Ezra 8.17)" and suggests, "Zechariah . . . was probably also a priest".[11]

Zechariah's prophetic preaching inspired those living in Judah and Jerusalem with great effect. The Temple was completed, "on the third day of the month of Adar, in the sixth year of the reign of King Darius".[12]

---

9 NRSV, 1412.
10 Zechariah was son of Berechiah (or 'Barachiah') son of Iddo. The omission of Berechiah in the Ezra locations does not negate the paternal lineage through him from Iddo.
11 *South Asia Bible Commentary* 1192.
12 Ezra 6.15, and given in the NRSV as 515BCE. See the notes regarding the interpretation of the specific dates for this between March and April of that year as per our calendar.

PART TWO

New Testament reference to Zechariah in Matthew's gospel reflects Matthew's confusion of two men, each with the same name. At Matthew 23.35, Zechariah "son of Barachiah" is given as having been murdered between the temple and the sanctuary, " . . . by command of the king they stoned him to death in the court of the house of the Lord".[13] Matthew has wrongly identified the man who was killed to be the prophet Zechariah son of Barachiah when in fact the person he is referring to is an earlier Zechariah, "son of the priest Jehoida". Luke 11.51 also notes this killing but does not make the same identity mistake.

How the Book of Zechariah is structured

As we have noted already, Zechariah is essentially in two parts. Chapters 9 – 14 reflect a more pessimistic later authorship. Chapters 1 – 8 are our focus.

In the first six chapters are eight visions that speak of how the people are to present themselves before God: purified and restored so as to set themselves a glorious future. Chapters 7 and 8 contain what are called 'oracles', namely messages that speak of the people 'returning to God' in expectation of His blessing upon them. Each prophetic utterance speaks in symbolic and metaphorical language about what God will do in the future as He brings His purposes into effect. It is clear that there is no linear chronology in what Zechariah says and that events far into the future, and events more closely at hand, are interspersed one amongst the other.

Themes that appear in the book comprise assurance of the future coming Messiah. Descriptions of the Messiah that are used are, 'the angel of the Lord', 'the righteous branch', 'the crucified Saviour', 'the future King-Priest', 'the suffering shepherd', and the one who 'will return in glory'. As and when the Messiah comes political power will cease to rule and the Messiah will judge right from wrong. In effect, this is what Solomon prayed for when he assumed kingship upon the death of his father, David.

Zechariah also addresses the rebuilding of Jerusalem. It had been razed to the ground by the Babylonians in 587BCE. Rebuilding began during the reign of King Darius of Persia (522 – 486BCE), under Zechariah's

---

13 see 2 Chronicles 24.21. The 'Zechariah' referred to in 2 Chronicles is from an earlier period than the prophet Zechariah in this Reading Companion. These are two separate men from different periods of Old Testament history.

influence, but then lapsed only to come to completion perhaps about 100 years later.[14]

If in the Book of Amos we heard dire warnings so in Zechariah we find comfort. Good relationship with God will be restored; sin will be removed; the land purified from evil arising from foreign despoilation; and God will come among and rule His people with protection and hope for blessings to come.

Historical Context

Authorisation for the rebuilding of the Temple in Jerusalem came from King Darius I of Persia taking as provenance an earlier scroll of King Cyrus commanding this should be done. The task would not be easy. Though the exiled people were returning 'home' to their promised land they had, in fact, little there that they could call home. There was next to no normality for them to return to let alone inhabit. It stands to the credit of Zechariah and, as we shall see, Haggai that they were the ones whose prophetic ministries overlapped and together led the way for that which needed to be begun, to be begun.

Zechariah's focus was upon the Jerusalem Temple as an expression of spiritual, national and personal authority for a people having returned from exile. They had come back to a city and a land without, what we might call, internal civic and religious governance. I will return to this very shortly.

Nonetheless, this was the context in which Haggai and Zechariah found themselves called to prophetic ministry. Haggai, slightly earlier, led initially and Zechariah moved alongside, as it were, with the reconstruction of the Temple already under way.

Zechariah could see clearly what had gone wrong those years before and what had led to the Temple and city being destroyed and the people exiled. New authority with an authentic Hebrew voice was needed in leadership to help ensure that the mistakes of the past and the trust extended by King Darius was not betrayed. Zechariah was spurred on to the present rebuilding of the Temple as a sign and symbol of unity and hope both immediately for the people then, as well as for the future and to which all should aspire.

---

14 Ezra 5.6ff refers.

The rebuilding of the Temple was by order of King Darius I. Whilst we have already stated this it should be clearly remembered that he was king of Persia and it was Persia which was the ruling authority in Jerusalem. The first Temple that had been built in Jerusalem had been under the authority of Solomon, king of Israel in the lineage of David. The people of the Hebrews now had to accustom themselves to a Temple outwith hundreds of years of Davidic monarchy. This was a new situation. Meyers asks the question:

> Could [the Hebrew people] countenance a temple without a king? Could internal rule be legitimate, resting on the temple and its leadership alone, without the historically predominant monarchic component of national life?[15]

Zechariah, through his ministry as prophet, supplied God's affirmative response. The monarchical line would re-establish at some end point as determined by God. The priesthood meanwhile would have extensive power and authority, legitimately given and accepted even though Persian control continued through established civil governors. It was through the prophetic political acumen of Zechariah (and Haggai) that the people transitioned from exile to rebuilding what had been lost. What was created was something that was in so many ways entirely novel. Meyers and Meyers summarise, "Both prophets succeeded in an unprecedented way in helping to reconcile the present circumstances with sacred traditions ... there was no turning back".[16] In short, had they failed or the people rebelled Persia was the mightiest power of the day. The consequences of failure were too great to contemplate.

Geographical Context

There is little doubt in my mind, having read significantly around this period of Hebrew history, that rule within the Persia Empire was regarded as having been good for the Hebrews.

It was the Persian Empire which, admittedly not immediately, but eventually permitted the Hebrew people to return to their home land from exile. Having done so it then allowed them to develop their own religious

---

15 Carol L. Meyers and Eric M. Meyers, *The Anchor Bible: Haggai, Zechariah 1 - 8*, (Doubleday, New York, 1987), xlii.
16 Meyers and Meyers, xliii.

culture around the rebuilt Temple (520 - 516BCE). Next the Persians sanctioned the rebuilding of the walls of the city of Jerusalem under the authority of Nehemiah (444BCE).

Though this period saw the Hebrew people asserting themselves in their new identity over against other nations and cultures nonetheless for them a geopolitical movement which began with the rebuilding of the Temple and the prophetic influence of Zechariah and Haggai was to have effect for centuries to come.

HAGGAI

Who was Haggai?

Early in the summer of 2022 I was asked to prepare an Advent programme for the three congregations that form the parish of St James', Waimea, Big Island, Hawai'i.

My plan for that Advent programme was a devotional introduction to the Old Testament readings mostly for Daily Prayer in the *Revised Common Lectionary*.[17] In advance I prepared daily expository notes based on those readings and upon my forty years' experience as a priest. David Stout added what have been recognised as extremely valuable prayers to each day's notes.

I was not aware when I prepared that programme how relevant the Book of Haggai would be to the congregation of St Columba's, Pa'auilo. It was a congregation that had faced closure for many years with its membership falling to eight. Under the expert leadership of the parish's three clergy it has grown and in the late summer of 2022 made the decision to commit to an expansion of $800k. Why is this relevant to the Book of Haggai? Haggai was called by God to build a house of worship. The Temple in Jerusalem had lain in ruins. Haggai was called to rebuild the Temple.[18]

For a worshipping community a place of worship is at its heart. The Hebrew people returning from exile needed a visible place to be at the heart of that faith so as to shape the people's identity. Haggai was called to be the one leading the people to rebuild what Solomon had had constructed those many years before.

Haggai was one of those returning from exile. His name, with connotations in Hebrew meaning 'procession' or 'festival', signals the desire that God planted in him to complete the rebuilding of the Temple so that the great festivals of the Hebrew people can once again take place in the

---

17 Year B readings were taken and, with adaptations and adjustments, are those which form this Reading Companion.
18 In addition to the new growth at Pa'auilo that I saw beginning whilst in Hawai'i a year further on, as this Reading Companion is published the congregation at St James Church, Waimea is also considering and committing to a huge development program, possibly of $5m. The relevance of Haggai's teaching becomes all the more real.

Jerusalem Temple. Ashkenaz Asif Khan, Principal of the Zarephath Bible Seminary, in Rawalpindi, Pakistan, aptly cites the Hindi saying in respect of Haggai, "Your name reflects the kind of work you will do"![19] Haggai, it would seem, was particularly single-minded in the task set for him.

We know little about him as a person. He is linked with Zechariah in the Book of Ezra (5.1 & 6.14) and though each does not refer to the other they were contemporaries, Haggai being the slightly earlier of the two.

How the Book of Haggai is structured

The first two verses of Chapter One set the scene, ". . . the word of the Lord came by the prophet Haggai . . . thus says the Lord of hosts . . ." It was spoken to Zerubbabel, son of Shealtiel, governor of Judah. The scene is completed at the end of the second chapter of this very short book as it looks with anticipation to a final consummation of all things, "On that day declares the Lord . . ." In other words, the book is framed between the two standards of God speaking of what must happen now in the rebuilding of the sacred Temple, and what will eventually come to pass when all earthly authorities come to an end. Worship of God here and now foreshadows what will in due time be pure worship in heaven unencumbered by human failing and failure. The Temple must stand as the sign and symbol of the heart of faith now and simultaneously so of what is to come.

There are four prophetic utterances ('oracles') in the Book of Haggai focussing on God's authority over kings and nations. It is this which has led Darius I of Persia to permit the rebuilding of the Jerusalem Temple and with it to release some devolved power from the Persian governor in Jerusalem to the Temple authorities. The four prophetic oracles begin, respectively, at 1.3, 2.3, 2.11 and 2.21b. The flow of the oracles is from the initial injunction to begin the Temple reconstruction through to the blessings which will flow from the celebrations at its dedication and the foreshadowing of what is to come at God's end-time of all things.

Whether Haggai saw the re-establishment of the Davidic monarchy to be contemporaneous with this end-time vision is unclear to me. I am led to think he was deliberately ambiguous on the matter.

---

19 *South Asia Bible Commentary*, 1186.

PART TWO

Historical Context

In conjunction with historical evidence from elsewhere in the Old Testament backed up by archaeological material the Book of Haggai can be dated very precisely.

The four oracles came to him in 520BCE all in the second year of King Darius. From 1.1, " . . . in the sixth month, on the first day of the month . . ." And from 2.1 " . . . in the seventh month, on the twenty-first day of the month . . ." From 2.10, "On the twenty-fourth day of the ninth month" and on the same day the fourth oracle is announced, 2.20.

With Persian overlordship remaining over Israel there was no hope, let alone opportunity, that the historic monarchy of Israel (from David to Solomon and onwards and into the divided kingdom, exile and its collapse) to be re-established. It stands therefore to the pragmatic expertise that Haggai, and with him Zechariah, could work within the constraints of being a province of Persia and yet establish an autonomous priesthood with its own authority structure in, and based around, a rebuilt Temple. In and through this Haggai and Zechariah were appealing to ancient premonarchic life of the Hebrew people and the new *realpolitik* the people found themselves in post-exile.

The effect of Haggai's words resound from 1.12-15 which conclude with, " . . . and [the people] came and worked on the house of the Lord of hosts, their God, on the twenty-fourth day . . . in the six month.

It might seem strange that Haggai and Zechariah could minister as prophets within the ruling hegemony of a foreign power rather than, as is often supposed of prophets, to speak against that power. And yet they did so. What is more, they convinced the people that this was the right course whilst at the same time praising the Persian governor, Zerubbabel, "On that day, says the Lord of hosts, I will take you, O Zerubbabel my servant, son of Shealtiel, says the Lord, and make you like a signet ring; for I have chosen you, says the Lord of hosts". (2.23) As Meyers and Meyers suggest, "Both prophets succeeded in an unprecedented way in helping to reconcile the present circumstances with sacred traditions . . . there was no turning back . . . the alternative was to oppose the mightiest power of the day . . ."[20]

Haggai had spoken against the peoples' reluctance to complete the

---

20 Meyers and Meyers, xliii.

Temple's rebuilding which, having been begun earlier, had lapsed. Fear of foreign invasion and thoughts of likely return to exile had overtaken their efforts resulting in the perceived need to build homes to live in. Haggai's message was as uncompromising as it was convincing. In short, the house of God must come first; then you can build houses for yourselves!

This does not come easy to our ears. Far too many times we hear of ecclesiastics, clerical and lay, as well as oratorically gifted evangelists persuading people to part with hard-earned and perhaps sparse money to give to the work of the church (of whatever denomination or hue). This might be for building new churches today. It might also be for the salary or stipend, or expenses, of the church's work force; especially perhaps those at the 'top' of the particular set-up. In today's world we must deplore this. The church must be the servant of the people under God. If this means privation and working from the perspective of poverty then so be it.

But at the time of Haggai things were different. Perspectives were different. The central place of the Jerusalem Temple for the people of the Hebrews was such that its place and position was central for the life of the Hebrew nation. If it were not in place the nation and each individual within it would be the sufferer. It was to this context that Haggai spoke.

However, and now returning to our own time, if the means and the werewithal to develop the church and Christian outreach into the community is there, and the life of worship has brought the church to this point, then it must be developed. This was what I found to be the case at St Columba's, Pa'auilo.

Moreover, Christian evangelism and outreach together with church growth must, in our day, be orientated towards the conjunction of worship with social outreach, personal community holiness and care for family, community and self. This is the *realpolitik* of churches today.

Geographical Context

In the period we are looking at it is impossible to separate political, religious, ethical factors from social norms and conventions. All of these, and more, form the historical reality of the time. Likewise the geographical circumstances of the region. All of these are factors that could form part of a very much wider study.

For the Hebrew people, returning from exile was a return to the land promised them by God. In this sense a significant part of their self-awareness as a people is therefore related to the land they were now re-inhabiting. It was a land that formed part of the much larger Persian empire of which the Persians, as a mighty force, were in control.

The governor of Israel was Zerubbabel. Under the authority of the local governors of Israel the King of Persia decreed that the Temple in Jerusalem should be rebuilt with the Hebrew people permitted to return to Jerusalem and their 'promised land'.

It would seem the Hebrews posed no threat or worry to the Persian king. Local autonomy was granted to the Jerusalem Temple priests and the diarchic rule by these religious and the civic authorities seeming to function well. That Haggai and Zechariah helped 'oil the wheels' for this to be so is beyond doubt. This arrangement was to serve the Hebrew people well for some considerable time to come.

ZEPHANIAH

Who was Zephaniah?

Zephaniah places his autograph in the first verse of the Old Testament book that bears his name. Unique among the prophets he traces his paternal lineage back four generations to his great-great-grandfather, Hezekiah. We might ask why he does so.

If this Hezekiah was the same person as the King Hezekiah it could be said that Zephaniah was seeking to give increased credence through historic provenance to the prophetic message to which he was giving voice. Hezekiah, as we have already noted, was a good king. In addition, Zephaniah might also have been stating that, because of this lineage, he had access to the royal courts of his day. However, the lineage does not state "*King* Hezekiah". Might this therefore indicate his great-great-grandfather was not the king? Or, conversely, might it suggest that he had no need to use the title 'king' as the name and the subsequent lineage would be sufficient for all who knew it to recognise it to be royal? Either way, the jury is out. The text of Zephaniah neither verifies or denies the suggestion that Zephaniah is of royal lineage from Hezekiah. Furthermore, there is no evidence to support either option elsewhere in the Old Testament. So, intriguing a possibility as Zephaniah's royal lineage might be, we accept the conclusion that it is not definite. Further evidence is needed. None is currently available.

The first verse of Zephaniah also tells us that "The word of the Lord..." came to him and did so during the reign of King Josiah of Judah. He ruled from 640 – 609BCE. Unsurprisingly, given what we have already noted from the other prophets within this Advent reader, we find Zephaniah finding fault with all in society for failures and flaws both within the religious observance of God and with governance of society. King Josiah was a reforming ruler and would have found ready support from Zephaniah as the latter gave forceful voice to the word that God spoke to him. It is likely that Zephaniah's prophetic message was given in the early years of Josiah's reign thus to give support to those reforms, political, religious and moral, that Josiah set in place. Further evidence in favour of this is the absence

PART TWO

of any reference to any reforms by Josiah suggesting, circumstantially, that they had yet to commence.

Officials and rulers had failed in their leadership and had "provoked the wrath of God". Nonetheless the "humble of the land" are "to seek the Lord" and to "seek righteousness" and "seek humility" so that "perhaps [they] will be sheltered on the day of the Lord's anger".[21] In the end of the day it is not the people themselves who will decide whether this will be so but God alone. Zephaniah is content to leave the final word of judgment to God and it is to God that all people must submit.

How the Book of Zephaniah is structured

As with other prophets Zephaniah alternates warning and judgment with hope and salvation for the faithful with a call to repentance in 2.1-3. He uses many turns of phrase that are also found in other prophetic writings with significantly suggestive parallels in Hosea, Isaiah, Amos and Micah and with definite allusions to turns of phrase in Habakkuk and Joel.[22] Whether these parallels originate in texts with which Zephaniah is familiar, or are drawn from familiar colloquial phraseology cannot be certain.

A theological feature is his message of "the day of the Lord". It appears twenty-three times in this fifty-three verse book. He uses the expression more than any other prophet. Walker notes how this phrase "ties the entire book together". The day of the Lord is variously, "near" (1.6, 1.14), a day of "wrath . . . distress and anguish . . . trouble and ruin . . . darkness and gloom . . . clouds and blackness . . . and battle cry." And all this because the people "have sinned against the Lord". (1.17)[23] Indicating how God will exact his anger and punishment against his chosen people who should have known better Zephaniah like the other writing prophets before him warns that God will choose the warlike nations surrounding Israel and Judah to bring about this punishment if the people do not repent.

Important in Zephaniah's schema is the image of the holy remnant of God's faithful people. Walker notes these images, "the remnant of the house of Judah" (2.7), "the remnant of my people", (2.9) and "the remnant

---

21 Larry L. Walker, 'Zephaniah', in Tremper Longman III and David E. Garland, eds, *The Expositor's Bible Commentary (Revised Edition), Daniel – Malachi*, 655 (citing Zephaniah 2.3, (Zondervan Academic, Grand Rapids, Michigan, USA, 2008).
22 Cf. Larry Walker, 654.
23 Ibid.

of Israel" (3.13). This remnant will constitute a new "chosen people, a royal priesthood, a holy nation, a people belonging to God".[24] Whilst Walker is citing, from the New Testament, 1 Peter 2.9, a striking parallel is to the later verses of Isaiah 6.

The opening verses of Isaiah 6 are regularly read at ordination and licensing services of ministers and priests into new spheres of ministry. Mostly the reading stops at verse eight. However if chapter six is continued through to the end it becomes increasingly dark and even foreboding. In it we read that proclaiming God's message to the people will result in their failure to comprehend and understand. It will, to paraphrase, 'make their mind dull and stop their ears, not see with their eyes and not be healed'. "What will be left of and for God will be a "holy seed", a "stump". (Isaiah 6.13). This is analogous to Zephaniah's 'remnant' for this is where the residue of uncorrupted faith is to be found and from which new life in God will form. Kent Harold Richards in the NRSV correctly considers that Zephaniah's prophecy of judgment is not "void of promise and hope".[25] In that sense our devotional reading of Zephaniah 3.1-14 in Part One of this book might, with profit, lead on to the message of hope that begins at 3.14 and continues to 3.20. Regarding the beginning and ending of Zephaniah, Walker summarises graphically and pointedly:

> The opening verses of Zephaniah contained [sic] some of the most vivid and graphic language found anywhere in Scripture. The entire universe is depicted as being overturned in judgment. In contrast, [the] closing verses contain some of the most moving descriptions of the love of God for his people found anywhere in Scripture.[26]

Zephaniah's style is highly and clearly unapologetically graphic; upsettingly so to modern day appeasers of those with tender dispositions or of a Christian understanding that God will excuse wrongdoing and wrongdoers!

Historical Context

Prior to King Josiah, the reigns of Manasseh (695-642BCE) and Amon (642-640BCE) had been dissolute and wicked. Whilst they had both

---

24 Walker, 655.
25 Kent Harold Richards, NRSV, 'Zephaniah', 1402.
26 Walker, 691.

remained loyal vassal subjects of Assyria, local insurgencies within Assyria from Babylon were distracting its governance of territories, including Judah. As a consequence Josiah was able to begin and continue his reforms at home in Judah and draw back divided territories in Israel, to the north.

What Josiah did was to purge foreign cults and practices, not least as Walker records, the destruction of Assyrian religious practises and their associated shrines along with the removal of their personnel. His methods involved significant force and perhaps little compassion in terms of redeploying the personnel whose livings and livelihoods were summarily ended. 2 Kings 22 & 23 is pertinent.[27] Principal to what Josiah did was the centralised return of worship to the temple in Jerusalem contemporaneous with the discovery of the Book of the Law in the temple.

Josiah's reforms were not to outlast him however, significant though they were to be in times to come. His immediate successors, following his death in battle in 609BCE, Jehoahaz and the puppet king Jehoiakim were both subservient to the Egyptian Pharaoh. They "did what was evil in the sight of the Lord" and as a consequence many of the warnings about which Zephaniah prophesied came to pass.

Geographical Context

Zephaniah's message from God, whilst generalised globally in his opening verses, was nonetheless principally for Judah. Reformation of the temple in Jerusalem was closely allied with prosperity and return to faithfulness in God in the region, the Hebrew lands, around it.

Surrounding nations are cited in Zephaniah 2.4-15 as representing the four points of the compass, respectively, Philistia (west, 2.4-7), Moab and Ammon (east, 2.8-11), Cush (ie Egypt, to the south, 2.12) and Assyria (to the north, 2.13-15). Each in different ways represent hostility to the Hebrew peoples.

Philistia and its five city-states (Gaza, Ashkelon, Ashdod, Ekron and Gath) was settled on the eastern shores of the Mediterranean. They were intent of maintaining and holding on to that land and coastline which they populated through sea-borne migration.

The people of Moab and Ammon were both hostile to the Israelites as a consequence of the earlier Hebrews' passage across their territories into

---

27 Walker, 653.

the land promised the Hebrews by God upon their escape from slavery in Egypt.

Cush, a general descriptive name referring in broad terms to Egypt, was a significant power, conquered and subdued by Nebuchadnezzar in 568BCE.

Assyria was the strongest political force of the time, though with instability rising as Josiah's reign continued in Judah. Not only did this instability help Josiah to establish his reforms but in due course it preceded the fall of the Assyrian Empire to Babylon in 612BCE. Thus, when Jerusalem fell, as foreseen by Zephaniah to be a consequence of the multiple and historic failures and flaws of the chosen people of God, it was to Babylon that the Hebrew top and middle ranking leadership were exiled.[28]

Having addressed his vituperative prophetic attack on the surrounding peoples, Zephaniah releases a stringent (3.1-8) indictment against Jerusalem. He had poured out his wrath against surrounding enemies up to this point and now spares nothing in what he says against Jerusalem. God's judgment upon the city and its people is unsparing. The unrepentant will be shown no mercy (3.1-8), but the faithful remnant (3.9-13) will be purified for they are the holy ones. Upon this there will then be a 'day of joy' (contrasting with Zephaniah's 'day of wrath' for example) in which the people, as "a new community of holy people" will be a blessing to all nations (3.14-20) who will join with them in true worship. Walker, again:

> The concluding verse (3.20) reiterates the Lord's promise to gather and bring his people home, where their fortunes will be restored and they will enjoy honor and praise from 'all the peoples of the earth'.[29]

---

28 Augustin Gnanachezhian's summary commentary on Zephaniah's indictments against these four surrounding peoples is especially helpful as it is upon Zephaniah's following indictment against Jerusalem. *South Asia Bible Commentary*, 1184 – 1185.
29 Walker, 692.

MALACHI

Who was Malachi?

This question can be put another way and in more contemporary format namely, "What's in a name?" Other prophets' names signify something that might relate or refer to their vocation as prophets. Thus Hosea and Isaiah, via the Hebrew root of their name, takes us in translation to 'salvation'. Joel means 'The Lord is God'; Obadiah 'servant of God' and Zechariah 'God remembers'. Malachi, and referring to 1.1 and 3.1, gives us the name in translation, 'my messenger'.

Since nothing else is said about Malachi as a person in the Old Testament, scholars suggest that what appears as an autograph may be little more than description of an otherwise unknown person, or even the introduction to a further section of the book of Zechariah.

Nonetheless, it is the case that with the other prophets we are looking at in this Advent reader there is extensive corroboration of who the prophets, our ancestors, were and when they were active. Evidence from elsewhere in the Old Testament and, in some cases, archaeological findings can be adduced for support. The respective books of 1 & 2 Chronicles, 1 & 2 Kings, Ezra, Nehemiah are all pertinent in their support of the dates and activity of the other prophets we have considered. Malachi, however, is an exception. We know nothing about him and there is no testimony, let alone definitive evidence in the Old Testament, as to when he was active.

Notwithstanding this questioning it is, in my view, reasonable to suppose Malachi was a person. The translation and meaning of his name, as such, is in the genre of how the other prophets' names can be understood. He was a messenger whose task was to signal the need for the people to be purified from wrongs and united in readiness for the day of the Lord's coming. Given that it was the temple priesthood which led the corruption Malachi's particular prophetic invective is directed towards them.

How the Book of Malachi is structured

Malachi is well written largely in prose style and is the product of a skilled hand familiar with dialogue and interrogative questioning.

Charges, in the form of rhetorical accusation, are placed before the hearers and readers of this text with similarly rhetorical questions then given such as might elicit shamed or repentant response. An example of this comes in 1.6ff:

> If then I am a father, where is the honor due to me? And if I am a master, where is the respect due me? Says the Lord of hosts to you, O priests who despise my name.

And considering failure of the priests to give due honour to God in their activity in the temple Malachi continues, 1.13b)

> "What weariness this is," you say, and you sniff at me, says the Lord of hosts. You bring what has been taken by violence or is lame or sick, and this you bring as your offering! Shall I accept that from your hand? Says the Lord.

In other words, the priests in the temple were deliberately bringing what was second best (or worse) in and to worship rather than the best that they could offer. Perhaps trivially, I recall a pastoral conversation where someone once said, in tones of deliberate disrespect concerning a fund-raising church sale, that she always gives, "the cheap things to the church". Her comment remains for me as a disturbing intrusive memory of disrespect to God.

Malachi also poses the charge that if the people really are the chosen people of God, bound in covenant relationship with God, why do they not behave as such.

As things are, Malachi looks forward to a final fruition of all things for the people of God's promise. This was not to prove the outcome for the people of the first covenant. However, the placing of Malachi as the final book of the Old Testament in all known versions of the scriptures found to date, enable it to point forwards to the coming of Christ as that salvation hope. Malachi again:

> See, I am sending my messenger to prepare the way before me, and the Lord whom you seek will suddenly come to his temple. The messenger of the covenant in whom you delight – indeed, he is coming, says the lord of hosts. (3.1)

The messenger who is to come will be like Malachi himself, someone pointing forward to an ultimate time when all things will be put right by God himself. Within Christian faith the messenger is John the Baptist.[30] John the Baptist is, in turn, the messenger and forerunner of the coming of Jesus who will announce that God's salvation has come to "this house today".

Historical Context

Malachi refers to activity in the Jerusalem temple, whether that of priests, or of sacrifices offered and other matters of temple service, together with fidelity as God's covenant people. He was clearly familiar with what was going on (in other words 'going wrong') in the temple. The fact that he identifies abuses within the temple and its priesthood (1.6-14 and 2.1-11) would indicate, at the very least, that the rebuilt temple had succumbed, variously, to laziness, malpractice and corruption. The temple being referred to would, of course, be the second temple. This means that Malachi can be dated some time after its rededication in 516 / 515BCE. The flaws and failings he identified would therefore have developed in the years subsequently. Can we pin down the date of Malachi's prophetic activity more accurately?

Neither Ezra or Nehemiah mention Malachi. Nor does he refer to them. Even though Nehemiah and Malachi were both concerned with marital divorce each had different questions regarding it; divorce between Jew and Gentile partners was the issue for Nehemiah whereas it was divorce between Jews that Malachi addressed. Had both Nehemiah and Malachi been both active at the same time one would quite reasonably expect that there would have been some cross-reference in respect of divorce as a related, even if differently directed, problem. There was no such cross reference. Accordingly I am led to recognise that they were not contemporary.

Eugene Merrill[31] proposes, "A date for Malachi at 480 – 470BC is not at all unreasonable". Earnest Nadeem[32] concludes, broadly in line with Merrill, a time between the "two tenures" Nehemiah undertook in Jerusalem. Such considerations seem fair to me. Others may feel differently. Of the matter we need say no more. It is beyond our remit.

---

30 Malachi 3.1 is cited at Matthew 11.10 and Mark 1.2 (where it is also conflated with material from Isaiah and Exodus).
31 Eugene H. Merrill, 'Malachi', in *The Expositor's Bible Commentary*, 841.
32 Earnest Nadeem, 'Malachi' *South Asia Bible Commentary*, 1203.

Geographical Context

We need not be detained long here either. Malachi was concerned with abuse being perpetrated by the temple leadership in Jerusalem. Malpractice in leadership adversely influences the behaviour of those who look to their leaders for guidance and to be an example to emulate. Where flawed behaviour becomes the established norm in leadership it is never long before bad behaviour 'trickles downward' into and amongst people at large with, typically, only a minority resisting the trend.

Malachi's concern was with such malpractice in the temple and in the community. His focus was Jerusalem, its temple leadership and for the wider Jerusalem community. For this reason we locate him, and his prophetic ministry, in Jerusalem and in general terms during the period we indicate above.

MICAH

Micah is the last of the 'minor prophets' in this daily cycle of readings for Advent. We have taken the decision to place one reading from him on the twenty-eighth day of Advent. This reading will therefore be omitted in those years when Advent is shorter.

Who was Micah?

The first verse of the Book of Micah gives the prophet's autograph, "The word of the Lord that came to Micah of Moresheth in the days of Kings Jotham, Ahaz and Hezekiah of Judah, which he saw concerning Samaria and Jerusalem."

Moresheth was a village some twenty-five miles south west of Jerusalem located in the rising land that links the coastal plain spreading inland from the Mediterranean Sea to Palestine's central range of higher hills. Though Micah therefore comes from the southern kingdom of Judah he neither spares criticism of Jerusalem with its flawed Temple and city leadership nor yet of Samaria in the north. The fall of Samaria in 722BCE is given as a warning as to what would in due course happen to Jerusalem.

Evidently casting modesty aside Micah tells us, "I am filled with power, with the spirit of the Lord, and with justice and might, to declare to Jacob his transgression and to Israel his sin". (3.8) There is no account, whether in the book Micah itself nor yet elsewhere in the Bible of Micah's call to prophetic ministry. Nonetheless we are told that what Micah said was exacted and enacted through 'lament and wailing, barefoot, naked and in mourning' (from 1.8 – 1.10) and conducted without requirement for payment. The name 'Micah' literally translates as an exclamation, rather than a question, "Who is like the Lord?"

Micah's message, driven by a strong ethical and religious stance, was of justice and right behaviour before God, "[The Lord] has told you, O mortal, what is good; and what does the Lord require of you but to do justice, and to love kindness, and to walk humbly with your God" (6.8). He railed against the deceit and hypocrisy of the wealthy and of the city leaders (6.9-12). Micah dared to speak of wrongdoing and did so, seemingly without fear or favour, of those who could do him harm. Truth-tellers in our day risk much by speaking out when, otherwise, silence would condone wrong. The courage of those who speak against wrongdoing stands as a significant witness and encouragement to us all similarly to do likewise most especially on behalf of those who are variously weak or who have been rendered powerless through wrongful exercise of authority. Ethical integrity and faithfulness towards God, right belief and social concern all go hand in hand. They did so in the time of Micah and they still do.

Micah is often cited as having come from the labouring classes, though the text (especially at 2.6-11) might also suggest his background was that of the agricultural "oppressed middle class".[33]

How the Book of Micah is structured

The text we have broadly consists of three cycles[34] each with the prophetic injunction, "Hear . . ." (1.2 opening the cycle of Chapters 1 – 2), "Listen . . ." (3.1b for the cycle in Chapters 3 – 5) and "Hear . . ." (6.1 for the cycle in Chapters 6 – 7). Each contains both warning with judgment and hope with justice.

Across Chapters 1 – 2 Israel's sin is given as that which brought about exile; with a faithful remnant remaining behind in ravaged Judah. Something similar is said in the second cycle where it is given that Jerusalem's flawed leadership will be punished and, "Zion shall be ploughed as a field; Jerusalem shall become a heap of ruins, and the mountain of the house [of the Lord] a wooded height." (3.12) But after the warning of destruction comes the promise of hope that is to be in a restored Jerusalem, "In days to come the mountain of the Lord's house shall be established as the highest of the mountains, and shall be raised up above the hills. People shall stream to it, and many nations shall come . . ." (4.1-2a) Failure in worship and devotion to God is pictured in the third cycle along with falsehood and wrongdoing despite the requirement from God to His people to do what

---

33 Bruce K. Waltke, 'Micah' in Thomas Edward McComiskey, *An Exegetical and Expository Commentary: The Minor Prophets II*, 1993, Baker Book House Company, Grand Rapids, Michigan, 594.

34 Scholarship does vary on this point. In support of the three-cycle structure Achtemeier (288) says, ". . . there is no doubt that the book exhibits a structure in which oracles of judgment and of salvation alternate. Thus, we find 1:2-2:11 (judgment) followed by 2:12-13 (salvation); 3:1-12 (judgment) followed by 4:1-5:15 (salvation); 6:1-7:7 (judgment) followed by 7:8-20 (salvation)".

the Lord requires, namely, " . . . to do justice and to love kindness and to walk humbly with your God." (6.8b)

Despite all that people do wrong, and against which Micah rails, God will in the end triumph.

In terms of technical detail Chapters 1 – 3 can be specifically accredited to Micah himself, with the remainder of the book being edited additions added by others concerned to extend and apply the message of Micah.

Historical Context

Micah, a contemporary of Amos, Hosea and Hezekiah prophesied during the reigns of Jotham, Ahaz and Hezekiah. It is generally felt by scholars that the particular prophetic oracles (the messages) in the book of Micah relate to particular historical events current at the time, though not exclusively so. This is because the whole of the book has an overarching purpose. It recalls God's ancient promise to the people. It laments subsequent failure and looks forward to the redeeming forgiveness of God who wills peace with justice held in the frame of faithfulness to God.

Overall, the book of Micah would appear to be a reflection upon some two centuries of God's promise to the Hebrew nation that it will be a light and standard bearer before the world. It was given ancient promise by God that this should be so. But woeful it is that the leadership of the people hinders God's purpose towards this end. Therefore the nation and its people will be punished. God will use other nations as instruments to enact this punishment and thereby make an example of the failed Hebrew leadership. In the end, however, God will triumph and will indeed make the Hebrew people the blessing of peace and justice to the nations that God intends.

Micah's prophetic activity can be dated from the reign of Jotham (742-735BCE) to Hezekiah (715-686BCE) with King Ahaz between them. To the east the Assyrian army, comprising professional soldiery paid for by levies raised from conquered and vassal states, was all-powerful and perpetually threatening.

The Hebrew leadership in the northern kingdom, Israel, was transported into exile with compliant foreigners placed in Israel to take the place of those deported. It was named Samaria and thus a province of Assyria. Incursions by the Assyrian army to quell Hebrew unrest persisted, most damaging of all being that into Judah in 701BCE.

Geographical Context

Assyrian intentions of conquering lands to the west and as far as the Mediterranean coast were realised onwards from around 745BCE when problems nearer home were variously resolved or subdued. Damascus fell in 732BCE. The northern kingdom succumbed to invasion by Shalmaneser the Assyrian emperor some ten years later, with its leadership taken into exile. Judah, for all intents and purposes already a vassal state of Assyria because King Ahaz had previously appealed to Assyria for protection against threat of incursion by other nations, was fully overtaken in 701BCE. The immediate circumstance causing this was King Hezekiah's refusal to pay the required levy, accepted by his predecessor Ahaz, to Assyria. All this, which Micah foresaw, came to pass.

BIBLIOGRAPHY

Elizabeth Achtemeier, *New International Biblical Commentary: Minor Prophets I*, Paternoster Press, Carlisle, UK, 1996.

The Big Book, Alcoholics Anonymous World Services Inc, 2001.

Alternative Prayer Book 1984, according to the use of The Church of Ireland, Collins Liturgical Publications, London, 1984.

The Book of Common Prayer, According to the use of The Episcopal Church (USA), The Church Hymnal Corporation, New York, 1979.

Rupert Bristow, *Only Connect: 150 prayers to aid reflection*, Kevin Mayhew, Buxhall, Suffolk, UK, 2009.

Avery Brooke, *Plain Prayers in a Complicated World*, Cowley Publications, Cambridge, Boston, Massachusetts, © Avery Brooke, 1993.

Daily Prayer and Psalter: additional Liturgical documents, Scottish Episcopal Church, undated but currently available both in paper format and as a download.

Winston Halapua, *Waves of God's Embrace: Sacred Perspectives from the Ocean*, Canterbury Press, Norwich, England, 2008.

Desmond Knowles, *Voicing A Thought On Sunday, Homilies and Prayers of the Faithful for the Three-Year Cycle*, The Columba Press, Blackrock, Co Dublin, Ireland, 1992.

George Mackay Brown, *Andrina and Other Stories*, Polygon, Edinburgh, 2010.

Kupuna Katherine Kamalukukui Maunakea, 'A Prayer for Leadership', in *Kupuna Maunakea's Book of Prayers, 4th Edition*, © The Katherine K. Maunakea Foundation, *1994, Nanakuli, Hawai'i.*

Eugene H. Merrill, 'Malachi', in Tremper Longman III and David E. Garland, eds, *The Expositor's Bible Commentary (Revised Edition), Daniel – Malachi*, Zondervan Academic, Grand Rapids, Michigan, USA, 2008.

Carol L. Meyers and Eric M. Meyers, *The Anchor Bible: Haggai, Zechariah 1 – 8*, Doubleday, New York, 1987.

Thomas Edward McComiskey, ed, *An Exegetical and Expository Commentary: The Minor Prophets II*, Baker Book House Company, Grand Rapids, Michigan, USA, 1993.

Prayer Book of The Episcopal Church in the USA.

Karl Rahner, *The Great Church Year: The Best of Karl Rahner's Homilies, Sermons and Meditations*, Herder & Herder, 1994.

Karl Rahner, *The Eternal Year*, Helicon Press Inc, 1st edn, 1964.

Saint Benedict's Prayer Book, Ampleforth Abbey Press, Ampleforth Abbey, York, England, sixth reprint 2011.

Christopher R. Seitz, *Interpretation: Isaiah 1 – 39*, John Knox Press, Louisville, Kentucky, 1993.

Larry L. Walker, 'Zephaniah', in Tremper Longman III and David E. Garland, eds, *The Expositor's Bible Commentary (Revised Edition), Daniel – Malachi*, Zondervan Academic, Grand Rapids, Michigan, USA, 2008.

Kahu Wendell Kalanikapuaenui Silva, 'Prayer for Inner Peace', *Hawaiian Prayers for Life Events*, Hawai'i Cultural Services [HCS], Kane'ohe, Hawai'i, 2020.

Walt Whitman *(1819 – 92), Passage to India*. (An epic poem cited as being in the public domain.)

Robert Louis Wilken, xiii, *Isaiah: Interpreted by Early Christian and Medieval Commentators*, trans. and ed. by Robert Louis Wilken with Angela Russell Christman and Michael J. Hollerich, William B. Erdmans Publishing Company, Grand Rapids, Michigan, 2007.

Brian Wintle, ed, *South Asia Bible Commentary*, Langham Partnership, Carlisle, UK, 2015.